NYMPH FISHING FOR
CHALK STREAM TROUT
&
MINOR TACTICS OF
THE CHALK STREAM

NYMPH FISHING
FOR
CHALK STREAM TROUT
&
MINOR TACTICS OF
THE CHALK STREAM

BY

G. E. M. SKUES

LONDON
ADAM & CHARLES BLACK

NYMPH FISHING FOR CHALK STREAM TROUT
FIRST PUBLISHED 1939
REPRINTED 1960

MINOR TACTICS OF THE CHALK STREAM
FIRST PUBLISHED 1910
SECOND EDITION 1914
THIRD EDITION 1924

THIS COMBINED VOLUME
FIRST PUBLISHED 1974
REPRINTED 1979

A. AND C. BLACK (PUBLISHERS) LIMITED
35 BEDFORD ROW, LONDON WC1R 4JH

© A. AND C. BLACK LIMITED 1974

ISBN 0 7136 1447 1

Printed in England by
Billing & Sons Limited, Guildford, London and Worcester

PART I
Nymph Fishing for Chalk Stream Trout
p. 1

PART II
Minor Tactics of the Chalk Stream
p. 139

NYMPH FISHING FOR
CHALK STREAM TROUT

DEDICATED TO

The NAIADS of WESSEX

Happy the man who, studying nature's laws,
From known effects can trace the secret cause.

> Whatever here I may declaim
> The very clever folk I sing to
> Will most indubitably cling to
> Their pet delusions all the same.

(With apologies to RUDYARD KIPLING)

CONTENTS

CHAP.		PAGE
I.	Apologia	1
II.	History and Evolution	3
III.	Definitions:	
	What is a Nymph?	9
	What is Nymph Fishing?	13
	Fish "In Position"	16
IV.	The Way of a Trout with a Nymph	17
V.	Rods and Gear	27
VI.	Fishing the Nymph	31
	and Mayfly Nymphs	48
VII.	Exceptions	49
VIII.	Personal	51
IX.	Reaction	61
X.	The Pronouncements of Halford	65
XI.	Pros and Cons	85
XII.	Hooks	91
XIII.	Hackles for Nymphs	93
XIV.	Dressing Methods	97
XV.	Patterns	109
XVI.	Bibliographical	119
	Index	129

NYMPH FISHING FOR CHALK STREAM TROUT

I

APOLOGIA

A GOOD many years ago I vowed by the Nine Gods—ineffectual beasts—that never again would I be guilty of a book. Years after, like a fool, I let myself be jockeyed against my better judgment into allowing the publication in book form of a collection of the angling oddments which from time to time I had committed to the periodical press. Some good man—I forget who it was—said *"Indignatio facit versus"*—and now in the beginning of my Eighties I find myself impelled by that same emotion to go back once more on my pledge to the Nine Gods.

In writing of the art of trout fishing with the fly, my contribution to knowledge has by degrees led, viâ the resuscitation of the use of the wet fly on chalk streams, to the practice of the use of life-like representations of the natural nymph. And while every fresh day's experience of the practice of nymph fishing has confirmed me in my conviction that I have been moving in the right direction, and while the practice appeared to find acceptance on almost every hand, I find in my latter days there seems to be a movement on foot designed to re-rivet on the chalk stream angler the fetters of dry-fly purism from which I thought common sense and the experience of the last quarter of a century had shaken him finally free.

Whether that movement be due to the revolt—in my opinion quite a legitimate revolt—on the part of a section of chalk stream anglers against the use by some anglers on chalk streams of lures supplied to them by—presumably ignorant—tackle dealers under the name of nymphs, but which bear no resemblance to the larval stage of the Ephemeroptera, to which alone the term "nymph" may legitimately be applied, or to some more obscure cause, I feel driven, in my old age, to attempt the task of describing fully and in detail what I conceive to be the true and proper practice of nymph fishing, and of establishing its justification. I shall no doubt fail to convince those who do not wish to be convinced, but at least I shall have done my best. If only I could persuade anglers to take out with them regularly a marrow scoop to extract the contents of the stomachs of their trout (without the dilatory and horrid mess of an autopsy), and a white-enamelled cup into which to wash out these contents, so as to analyse them and see what the trout are really eating, I might have some hope, for they would learn when the trout are taking winged flies and when nymphs and what nymphs are really like, and realise the justification of nymph fishing as a valuable branch of the chalk stream angler's art.

I am conscious that the volume contains a number of repetitions, but I have had to choose between making them and crippling my argument by innumerable cross-references. So I pray the forgiveness of my readers.

G. E. M. S.

II

HISTORY AND EVOLUTION

It may perhaps be recognised as desirable that I should set out historically how nymph fishing has developed out of the old art of wet-fly fishing as practised by our forebears on chalk streams.

Before the dry fly became dominant on chalk streams two or more flies were used on a cast, and there can be little doubt that in still weather it was found difficult, if not impossible, for really good chalk stream trout to be taken with the wet fly on account of drag, and that to achieve success a definite ruffle was necessary. The angling books from Cotton onward give few clues to enable one to comprehend the methods employed, but one infers that the flies of those days must have been cast more or less downstream. The best authority that can be quoted on the subject is to be found in the *Diary of a Test Fisherman* (the Rev. Richard Durnford) covering the years 1809 to 1819, and published in 1911 by Mr Henry Nicoll. From this record it appears that little success was possible on chalk streams without a fairly strong breeze—sometimes described by the diarist as a "whistling wind", at other times as a "sufficient" wind. The Diary gives little information to guide one as to whether the fishing was up-stream or down or across, but it may be inferred that it was more often down and across or down than otherwise but invariably with the wind. The type of rod then favoured (long and soft in action) necessitated fishing with the wind. Yet substantial success was recorded on most of the occasions which took the Reverend diarist to the waterside. On many occasions he mentions that a Caperer or bob fly was necessary "to steady the cast". And on several occasions he refers to the throats of the trout being full of the "nymphae of the gnats ascending through the water before they take wing". So far as I know this is the only record of pre-dry-fly times which indicates that the angler realised that his fish were taking the natural insect in that stage. The patterns of artificial fly illustrated in the Diary suggest that the fly was taken for an up-winged dun in the act of hatching. Col. Peter Hawker, a mighty Test angler of the beginning of the 19th century, always fished two flies down-stream. It seems that at that period of angling history, when trout were taking duns at the surface the artificial fly was considered useless except on rough and windy days, and anglers either stayed at home or used minnows or the cross line. The flies tied to gut which were used on the Itchen in the middle 'seventies when I was a boy at Winchester were more nymph-like in shape than the Rev. Richard Durnford's patterns, though they were supposed to be, and in fact were, used dry. And it was not until H. S. Hall had evolved the eyed hook for floating flies, and with it worked out the method of winging split-winged floaters, that the old type of fly was abandoned on chalk streams. For the old type see illustration at the head of the frontispiece. It is still in use for down-stream fishing on many rough rivers, having what is known as "a good entry". The dry fly was not hinted at in angling literature until 1841— (G. P. R. Pulman, *Angler's Vade-Mecum*, 1841 and 1846)— and was first definitely described in the same author's Third Edition, 1851. It was however in use on the Itchen before 1857, for it is described in the *Field* that year by Francis

HISTORY AND EVOLUTION

Francis as an established institution on that river, though he says "on rough windy days they get drowned and trout will take the wet fly as well as a dry one or even better". Halford found the dry fly established on the Wandle in 1867. It was definitely dominant on the Itchen when I was at Winchester as a boy in 1875. Curiously, the dry fly is not mentioned in the records of the Houghton Club down to 1908, though it must have been in use in the 'eighties, but fishing with the cross line and the blow line went on on the Test long after they had been abandoned on other chalk streams in favour of the floating fly.

G. S. Marryat, who was probably the greatest expert with the dry fly that ever lived, was brought up on the Dorsetshire Frome and fished it with the wet fly downstream in his youth. He returned from Australia in or about the 'seventies, but when Halford and he met in John Hammond's shop at Winchester in 1879 he was already the finished expert with the dry fly. It was however only in that year that he came into touch with H. S. Hall who was then elaborating his famous patterns of the eyed hook, and they worked out together the early methods of dressing the split winged floater.

Soon afterwards, in 1885, H. S. Hall wrote of the dry fly in the Badminton Library and shortly afterwards (in 1886) F. M. Halford's *Floating Flies and how to Dress Them* was published, followed early in 1889 by *Dry Fly Fishing in Theory and Practice*, after which the dry fly on chalk streams became at first a rage and then a religion.

Quite naturally it was contrasted with the only method previously in use on chalk streams (if we exclude the cross line and the blow line), viz. the wet fly fished with the wind and in general down-stream and searching the water. It became the fashion for dry-fly fishers to speak disparagingly of their immediate predecessors. They were represented as clumsy floggers of the water. Many no doubt deserved this reproach, but there must have been some extremely clever anglers among them. The dominant feature of dry-fly fishing was the casting of the floating fly up-stream to individual fish, and it had the great merit that it could be done in calm and bright weather—which was an impossibility for the down-stream dragging fly. Then for many years it does not seem to have occurred to anyone to try casting the wet fly up-stream to individual fish, and that it too could be done in calm and bright weather, and F. M. Halford does not seem even to have suspected that it could be done. Indeed the heavy tapered oiled silk lines and the powerful and heavy split-cane rods then deemed necessary for dry-fly fishing were quite unsuitable for delivering a wet fly to an individual fish, especially against a wind. No doubt a few anglers here and there used a wet fly on chalk streams and caught fish, but, so far as any record goes, without reasoning out the justifications for their methods. Indeed from first to last and down to to-day the ignorance of the vast majority of even highly-experienced anglers of the very existence of the nymph, its form and character, is astonishing. Similarly the vast majority of chalk stream anglers (Halford among them) kept on casting a succession of dry flies to feeding trout which were seen to be breaking the surface, most of such anglers being wholly unconscious that for hours and days at a time these trout were feeding on nymphs and were letting the natural hatched-out insect go by. Still when all was said and done the dry fly came in because in conditions often prevalent on chalk streams it made the catching of trout easier. For years I was equally unconscious. But in the later 'nineties the difficulty of inducing bulging trout to take the floating

HISTORY AND EVOLUTION

fly, combined with the obvious fact that they were feeding on nymphs, led me (and no doubt others) to experiment on bulgers with patterns of wet flies which were successful on rough North Country streams where trout were seldom seen to break the surface, and to cast these flies up-stream to the bulging fish.

From this beginning there naturally came to my mind the question, why, if the wet fly on chalk streams had brought great baskets in the past, it should have lost its efficacy with the advent of the dry fly. I had no desire (and indeed no need) to search the water by random casting. Trout rose too freely in the chalk streams which I fished to render such searching necessary; and I soon found that there were occasions when the winged wet fly, cast up-stream to feeding fish, was quite efficacious, though it was a long time before I realised that these occasions occurred nearly always when the trout were nymphing and not taking the floating fly.

I had supposed for a long time that the wet fly was taken on these occasions for a nymph in the very act of hatching. But after a while the presence in the mouths of some of my captures of nymphs with no show of wing led me to experiment with short hackled patterns dressed to imitate nymphs, and by 1910 when my first volume, *Minor Tactics of the Chalk Stream*, was published, though it dealt in the main with the use of the up-stream wet fly cast to individual fish, I had dressed and tried with some success a small series of nymphal patterns, fishing them in calm and bright weather like floating flies, but under water. In the succeeding eleven years I had made other attempts to represent nymphs—but I was hampered by the need to carry out hateful and messy autopsies to ascertain on what my trout were feeding, until towards the end of that period I was struck with the idea of using a marrow scoop to extract the contents of the trout's stomach in a single operation. The method proved completely successful, and time after time I was amazed to see what a huge proportion of these contents were nymphs—and how few were the winged flies. From this I moved on to the device of washing out these contents into a deep heavy white china plate (a baby plate proved ideal for the purpose); and, having it with the insects floating therein by my side on my fly-dressing table, I was able to dress (and compare in the water by the side of the natural insects) representations of the nymphs I had extracted, resembling them in size, contour, proportions and colour. I did not need to use these patterns when the trout were feeding on the surface, for then the dry fly was at once easier and more effective—but on those many occasions when the trout have been devoting their attention to the nymph and neglecting the floating fly I have found the appropriate pattern of nymph great medicine, however bright the weather and however smooth the water.

I have not hesitated, therefore, to do my best to let others share the benefit of my labours—being convinced that without any challenge to the merits of dry-fly fishing in its proper place I have evolved methods which are often effective where it fails.

III

DEFINITIONS

WHAT IS A NYMPH?

THE term nymph for the purposes of this little volume denotes a larva of one or other of the Ephemeroptera which has reached a stage in its growth when the cases on its shoulders containing the growing wings have become obvious. For the benefit of those anglers who are not aware of the life-history of the Ephemeroptera let me explain that the eggs of the perfect females of the Ephemeroptera are dropped or laid in the water, where in due course they hatch out as larvae and go through a series of under-water stages in weeds or mud or sand, eventually developing on their thorax cases which contain the wings which are only unfolded when the insect leaves the water for the air. In the final subaqueous stages the shape of the insects, apart from the wings and apart from the length of the setae, is very much what it will assume when hatched out into the air.

An artificial nymph is a pattern dressed on a hook to attract trout and grayling, and representing in size, colour and appearance one or other of the types of natural nymph. No artificial lure or fancy fly has a nymphal stage in its development, and it follows that there can be no nymph of the Bloody Butcher, the Professor, the Grizzly King, the Wickham's Fancy, nor any other fancy fly. Nor can beetles, with or without long whisks like the Spinners of up-winged duns; nor can hairy and shapeless objects, bearing no resemblance to natural nymphs, be properly classed as artificial nymphs; nor can artificial flies, hackled either profusely or lightly with full-sized hackles, be so classed. The latter types, in my judgment, where they suggest any insect at all, represent flies wrecked by stream or wave, raindrop or wind, generally in the moment of hatching, and they owe their attraction to the mobility of their hackles in the water. The others are frankly nothing but lures, no better in any respect than salmon flies, sea-trout flies, Alexandras, Demons, and other fancy patterns which are justly barred on chalk streams as illegitimate. The only type of pattern properly and justly called an artificial nymph is like in colour, dimensions, outline and proportion to a natural nymph of one or other of the Ephemeroptera; and the use of any of the other types, which I have classed as illegitimate, on chalk streams under the title of nymph only serves to discredit the true art of nymph fishing and to lend a handle to these dry-fly fanatics (and there are such) who want to put back the clock and re-establish the rigid and exclusive despotism of the dry fly.

From an examination of the stomach contents of a trout which has been feeding on natural nymphs, it may be seen that nymphs have only short legs and that there is no excuse for representing them with long hackles, like North Country hackled wet flies. These latter are sometimes said to represent nymphs—but they can only do so if fished dragging down-stream so that the hackles closely clasp the body—but this method of fishing is one which I would bar as involving casting at random and searching the water and as leading to catching or pricking undersized fish. Artificial nymphs, properly understood, have not silver bodies and scarlet legs like the Bloody Butcher. They have modest little wing cases on the thorax which do *not* extend all down the back, like the wing cases of a beetle. They are

DEFINITIONS

not long haired, though many have branchiae or breathing processes at their sides. They have very short whisks, which do not extend from the tail like the long whisks of Imagines. They have neatly tapered bodies (mainly translucent) with opaque thorax and often a definitely coloured head which may be suggested in the artificial representation by the exposed tying silk.

Later on in this volume I shall be giving dressings of nymphs which I have found successful on the Itchen and elsewhere—but I may say at once that I am not laying down these dressings as standards or attempting to stereotype patterns. On the contrary, they are merely illustrations, and I would have the angler make his own representations. Several times each year I find myself producing some new and often successful pattern to simulate in colour, shape and dimensions the natural nymphs which I have freshly extracted from the maw of the day's trout, to find my profit in the next day's or maybe the next weekend's basket.

Tackle dealers in general, wholesale or retail, with few exceptions (of whom Mr Roger Woolley of Hatton, Derby, and Mr T. J. Hanna of Stonard Street, Moneymore, Co. Derry, are bright examples), make little effort at genuine representations of the natural nymph. Indeed it is difficult to believe that most of them ever saw a natural nymph or have any notion of what it is like. But, while purporting to cater for the demand for nymphs they produce and sell a series of lures bearing little or no resemblance to the natural nymph, but which may at times in favourable conditions prove effective in taking occasional trout in much the same way as the sea-trout fly, the small Salmon fly and the Alexandra—all rightly barred on chalk streams.

With such lures I beg the would-be nymph fisher to have

nothing to do. Let him study the natural nymph as taken from the crops of trout on capture, and dress representations if he can do so, or at any rate get them dressed by some conscientious fly-dresser. The dressing of nymph patterns, as I shall show later, is a comparatively simple matter, and it constitutes an additional pleasure, to be enjoyed by the angler, which need not be despised.

The angling press, if only it were so disposed, might do much to promote a proper understanding of what nymphs really are and how their representations should be dressed, and to discourage the application of that title by tackle dealers to lures like beetles with long whisks and to numerous other confections which bear no resemblance whatever to the natural insect. If they would do this they would deprive anglers using these illegitimate objects on chalk streams of the excuse, "Oh, I bought this of Messrs Blank as a nymph". These lures only cast an undeserved discredit on the practice of legitimate nymph fishing.

I should like those who have been tempted into buying those alleged nymphs from tackle dealers to compare them with the natural nymphs newly extracted from the belly of a trout and to learn to know better.

Those who have been putting on the market the monstrosities of which I complain have not—or at least are not entitled to claim—even Dr Johnson's excuse, "Ignorance—sheer Ignorance, Madam"; for the books of Halford and Mosely—long ago angling classics—contain illustrations of the natural nymph which deprive them of that excuse. Members of the Fly Fishers' Club, with its cabinet of natural insects collected and preserved by F. M. Halford and Martin E. Mosely, have even less excuse for ignorance. But anglers may be assured that so long as their own ignorance and idleness enables them to be fooled, fooled they will be.

DEFINITIONS

WHAT IS NYMPH FISHING?

In this work then nymph fishing must, please, be understood to mean the art of taking trout or grayling at or under the surface with an artificial pattern credibly representing in colour, dimensions and outline a natural nymph of a type being accepted by trout and grayling on the stream which is being fished, and designed to be taken by the fish as such, and presenting such patterns to the trout in conditions to deceive them into believing them to be natural nymphs brought to them by the current.

Nymph fishing is not a sport by itself. It is auxiliary to the floating fly. It is a method, just as was and is the use of the wet fly on chalk streams, of taking trout and grayling which are not rising to the floating natural insect but are feeding. It is a method of presenting to the fish in these conditions representations of the food on which they are actually feeding far more precise than the wet fly (which at best *may* be taken for a hatching nymph) and not less, but probably more, exact than floating artificial flies are of the floating natural duns—or spinners. And just as the time to present the floating fly to the fish is when they are taking natural flies on the surface—so are the times to offer the fish an artificial nymph the hours, often prolonged, in which they are feeding wholly or mainly on the natural nymph. To my mind it is no more ethical (*i.e.* fair to other anglers and to the fishing) to hammer a nymphing fish with floating flies than to pester a surface-feeding fish with artificial nymphs. Indeed it is less so, for the persistently-presented floater, however well presented, is more likely to scare and put down a nymphing fish than an artificial nymph, even less well presented, is likely to scare a surface-feeding trout. And on the whole there is a slightly better chance of an artificial nymph taking a surface-feeding trout than of a floating artificial taking a nymphing fish. That is my experience, resulting from years of practice of both methods.

Nymph fishing is a comparatively new art, or perhaps it would be fairer to say a new phase of an old and largely forgotten art that has developed on chalk streams during the present century. The old art was the art of the wet fly as practised on chalk streams for centuries before the advent of the dry fly led, through the work of F. M. Halford, George Selwyn Marryat and others, to the supersession on chalk streams of the older method by the new, and for a while to the complete and exclusive dominance of the latter. The dry fly became a sort of religion and any attempt to revert to the older practice was regarded as a sort of sin against the Holy Ghost for which there was no remission. A few men however, natural born heretics no doubt, being of the detached order of intellect, came in time to wonder why the old art which had for centuries served our forefathers so well should have ceased to be effective and to have any merits, and they began to experiment by adapting to wet-fly fishing the new dry-fly method of casting the fly to individual rising fish, and they attained a degree of success which became embarrassing to the stern upholders of the strict faith of the dry fly. The practice led these heretics to enquire how it came about that trout were willing to accept winged flies under water; and, aided by autopsies as advocated by Halford, they became aware of a fact of which Halford was well aware, but the moral of which he had failed to appreciate, that rising trout fed more on nymphs than on their floating hatched-out subimagines. To this day it is probable that comparatively few of the enormous number of fishers with the fly are aware of this fact or of its bearing on the art of fly fishing and fewer still have any idea of what a natural nymph is like. But these

DEFINITIONS

wicked heretics decided that if the trout were willing, as for centuries they had proved themselves, to take winged artificial flies under water, it was not improbable that they would be still more willing in similar conditions (despite Halford's pronouncements to the contrary) to take under water well-conceived patterns representing as faithfully as possible the larval forms on which they were for the time being feeding, and that these patterns, like the wet flies with which these sinners had been previously experimenting, could be presented to the individual trout with all the pomp and circumstance of accuracy and avoidance of undersized fish which had been hitherto the exclusive privilege of the floating fly. Much to the chagrin of the archpurists, these heretics proved to be right, and by degrees a small school of fishers of chalk streams with the artificial nymph began to invade the most sacred stretches of the Hampshire rivers and their practice even extended to other rivers, such as the Usk, which had not been sacred to the dry fly. But I must emphasise the fact that, just as in *Minor Tactics of the Chalk Stream* I did not advocate, and indeed definitely disapproved of, what Halford termed fishing the water, but did advocate fishing the wet fly to the individual subaqueously feeding fish, in my advocacy of the use of the nymph on appropriate occasions, I apply precisely the same principles in practice. It is therefore out of place to cite against me the practices of the uninitiated anglers who fish the water with the nymph, searching it with a dragging nymph and taking or pricking and scaring unsizable fish.

Fish "in Position"

At page 130 of *The Dry Fly Man's Handbook* Halford gives a definition of a fish in position the first sentence of which

I can adopt without qualification:

When a trout has poised itself near the surface and is steadily taking duns or other flies without any great movement laterally or up or down the stream, it is said to be *in position*. When a fish in position is lying close to the bank and is rising freely, the angler on the same bank has found one under ideal conditions for the dry-fly fisherman, and may confidently expect a rise to his fly, if he is using the right pattern and succeeds in presenting it at the right moment and in such a way that the fish does not realize that it is being fished for, and its suspicions are, therefore, not aroused.

As to the second part I find it necessary to qualify what Halford says as follows: "the angler has found a fish in ideal conditions for the dry fly *or the nymph, according to what the fish may be taking at the moment*". With that qualification I can accept the rest of the paragraph. It will be noted, however, that Halford entirely ignores, both here and throughout the volume, the frequent occasions when the trout is equally in position but is *not* taking duns and *is* taking nymphs. In this connection I am not alluding to the occasions where trout are bulging.

IV

THE WAY OF A TROUT WITH A NYMPH

THERE are two states in which the natural nymph is taken by the trout—first in the active larval stage and second (and to the angler far more important) in the practically inert stage in which the mature nymph arriving at the surface to split its final nymphal envelope and to emerge as a subimago often reaches them.

The active nymphs may be routed out and pursued by the trout from their shelter in weeds or silt. This may be done in water so deep as to afford no clue or opportunity to the angler. In shallower water it is apt to produce the evidence of activity known as tailing, giving the angler a fairly precise indication where he may cast to his fish, but the opportunities thus afforded are few and the angler is handicapped by the fact that the natural nymphs which the trout are pursuing are in one or other of their active stages and cannot be accurately represented in action.

Where trout are bulging in the correct sense of the word (*i.e.* rushing about over weeds in comparatively shallow water, pursuing nymphs which emerge from their shelter in weeds, and making a bulge in turning as each nymph is captured), the nymph may be more or less active or it may be almost inert. In his chapter on "Nymphs and Bulgers" in *Fly Fishing: Some New Arts and Mysteries* (1915) Dr Mottram gives an interesting description of what he had observed on occasions when trout were bulging to nymphs. He writes:

The nymph may be seen coming down-stream, but often diverging to one side or the other, at the same time rising slowly to the surface: the motion is quite slow and even, not in the least fast or jerky, and a bulging fish, although he is quiet in his motions, is obviously not chasing nymphs but moving now to this side, now to that, in order to meet the nymph coming down.

He regards the nymph at this stage as swimming—and I think he is probably right, for I have so often seen trout bulging furiously over weeds, as if the nymphs emerging from shelter were numerous, while the hatch of subimagines is scanty or almost non-existent; so that it seems as if there were occasions when the nymph emerged and, if uncaptured by the trout, remained active enough to return to its fastnesses or to take refuge in others. Moreover, according to Dr Mottram the trout in these conditions is prone to take a dragging artificial nymph, a fact which rather suggests that he is in pursuit of nymphs of which some at any rate show a degree of activity.

There is another occasion on which the active nymphs may be taken, viz. after weed-cutting, when the nymphs, feeling their weed homes cut away from their stalks, seek shelter in bays and eddies under the banks—and are there found by the trout. Often, too, when cut floating weeds are coming down-stream trout may be seen rising among them —undoubtedly taking the active nymphs which are deserting or drifting out of the cut weeds.

The commonest occasion known in which the trout feeds on the nymph on its way to hatch is when he lies in position under a bank or in a run, poised to meet and accept without excitement or pursuit the mature nymphs brought to him helpless by the current. On such occasions it is often extremely difficult for the angler to detect whether the fish is taking nymph or subimago, for there may be, and often is, a string of hatched duns coming over him on the same line of current as brings the nymphs. Yet quite frequently the fish will be found to be taking the nymph to the exclusion of the winged dun, and that for hours at a time.

Dr Mottram on his next page makes a distinction between the swimming nymph and the floating nymph which I call the inert nymph, and describes the way in which fish take the latter:

> The fish is taking just beneath the surface of the water nymphs which are floating down and about to burst their cases in order to change into duns.

He calls the fish thus feeding on floating nymphs a dimpling fish in contradistinction from the bulger, feeding on swimming nymphs. He adds a little later of the floating nymph: "In this position they are motionless with legs and tail extended in the position of rest".

At times during a hatch of duns, trout, often large, may be seen questing about near the surface in mid-stream and taking the nymphs which are ascending from the river-bed as they find them, generally breaking or humping the surface when they effect a capture. And occasionally trout, when in the height of condition, may be observed hovering in the fastest part of the stream, not moving far from one spot and intercepting just below the surface the nymphs on their way to hatch, and at times doing so without breaking the surface.

It will thus be seen that the occasions most favourable to the angler fishing to individual selected fish are those when he is taking the mature and, for the moment, practically inert nymph on its way to hatch.

As a matter of fact it does not seem to have been realised for many years after the advent of the dry fly what a large proportion of the rising of trout under banks, and indeed in the open (other than bulging), is to nymphs on their way to the surface to hatch, with the result that many a fish so rising has been vainly hammered by anglers with floating flies.

The due appreciation of *how* a trout is rising forms the very essence of fishing, whether it be with floating fly or artificial nymph—and it is often no easy matter.

I have been assured on authority, which I will quote later on, from Mr Martin E. Mosely and Mr F. S. K. Pentelow (1) that the nymph coming to the surface is not inert but active, and (2) that it is not helped to the surface by being distended by some gas or lubricant, as I ignorantly inferred from my thirty years' experience of catching trout in the conditions above described with artificial nymphs. I propose therefore to give the reasons which led me to my conclusions.

I find Halford in *Dry Fly Fishing* in the chapter on Bulging distinguishing mature nymphs from immature partly by the fact that the former float.

After having opened his trout and turned the undigested portion of the contents of its stomach into a vessel of water, Halford proceeds (p. 233):

> The first thing that will strike the observant student is that one portion of the food is lighter than water, and, therefore, floating on the surface, but that a far larger proportion is of greater specific gravity and hence sinks to the bottom. The floating portion consists of winged insects and nymphae just on the point of assuming the winged state. It may fairly be asked how this last fact can be ascertained, and anyone taking the trouble can easily prove the question to his own satisfaction. Let him take two or three of the floating nymphae and as many of the sunk ones, and soak them for a few minutes in water in which is dissolved a small piece of ordinary washing soda . . . to counteract the action of the digestive fluid which is strongly acid. . . .

THE WAY OF A TROUT WITH A NYMPH

And after describing a process to bring about transparency, he proceeds on page 234:

A great contrast will be at once apparent between those that floated and those that sank. In everyone that floated it will be seen that inside the setae or tail of the nymph are plainly visible the setae of the subimago which is just about emerging from it; and in the same way, in each of the six legs, in the head, in each antenna and even in the abdomen itself the distinct outline with every detail of the corresponding limb or organ of the subimago may be seen.

In fact, in general appearance the nymph consists of two distinct portions, the inner or solid-looking portion being the subimago complete in all its parts, excepting that the wings are folded up inside a pair of somewhat oval-shaped wing covers; this subimago is, however, entirely enveloped in a thin transparent covering which is perceptibly larger than and projects beyond the outline of the insect itself. Attached to this apparently loose covering are all the organs which are especially provided for the larvae living in the water and not required for its subsequent or winged stage, and these organs are, without exception, shed with the larval envelope. . . . The less developed nymphs which sank in the water, when the autopsy was originally performed have, however, quite a different appearance. There is little or no appearance of the larval covering being loose; the setae and legs are solid-looking limbs, the latter often armed with formidable claws . . . in fact, there is no indication of an impending metamorphosis. In considering the deductions to be drawn from the comparison between the proportionate quantity of sunk and floating nymphs from the autopsy it must be remembered that all of the floating specimens were nymphae rising to the surface for the purpose of emerging from the envelope in the subimago stage, while the sunk ones were down among the gravel and must be considered as bottom food.

At this stage it may not be out of place to note that I deduced from the paragraphs quoted (1) that "nymph" about to hatch must have the envelope distended with a view to its splitting when relieved of water pressure on attaining the surface and with the preliminary object of helping to bring it to the surface, and (2) that in its ascent to the surface the nymph is comparatively inactive. I did not profess to know whether the distension be due to gas developed within the envelope or to some light lubricant, facilitating eclosion. If however (as appears to be the case) the mature nymph floats, it is not very material to the argument to establish what makes it do so.

I find Dr Mottram describing the mature nymph taken by the trout just under the surface as "floating" and "motionless" (entirely in accord with my experience). Then the three authors of the Lonsdale Book on *River Management* say that trout often "take nymphs floating at the surface". And I would respectfully invite those who challenge my suggested explanation of the distension of the nymph about to hatch to explain how otherwise the bulk of the nymph about to hatch could be increased without increase of weight so as to bring about a decrease of specific gravity leading to flotation. On the question of the inertness of the hatching nymph I had however, independently of Dr Mottram and before the publication of the passages quoted from his book, long come to the conclusion on my own observation that the mature nymph at the stage when nearing the surface to hatch *is* practically inert, having caught scores of good fish feeding subaqueously in position with artificial nymphs which made no pretence of imitating the motions of an active nymph, and this in despite of Halford's dictum at pages 144 and 145 of *Dry Fly Fishing*, that the trout will not look at it. Here the reason given by Halford for the alleged non-success of the artificial nymph is the supposed activity of the natural nymph. (I am told he used to quote Marryat as saying frequently, "You can imitate the nymph but you cannot imitate its wriggle"—but I would point out that his experiment with the nymphs extracted from a handful of

THE WAY OF A TROUT WITH A NYMPH

weed from the bed of the river is fallacious, as of course the nymphae from the weeds at the bed of the river would be active.) But that does not prevent an entirely different state of things from prevailing when the nymph is nearing the surface, about in a few moments to split its integument and emerge as a subimago. And I infer in despite of anything said to the contrary, that the nymph in such conditions is correctly described by Dr Mottram as motionless, and that there is therefore no need to imitate its then non-existent wriggle—and that a well-dressed imitation does *not* look unnatural to the trout feeding subaqueously.

Further grounds for believing the mature nymph to be practically inert when on its way to hatch out were (1) that it is rare—indeed practically unknown[1]—to find an active nymph in the maw of a trout taken in such conditions; (2) that the nymphing trout may be observed, particularly when under a bank, intercepting the nymphs brought to him by the current without excitement or pursuit such as one might expect if the nymph were active and able to try to escape—such pursuit indeed as one sees when a tailing trout follows and catches—or misses—a nymph or shrimp which he has routed out of the weeds.

It is moreover—it seems to me—not unreasonable to suppose that at the moment when a nymph comes up to hatch he secretes within his nymphal envelope a liquid or gas which by distending his shuck and increasing his bulk without adding to his weight assists his progress to the surface, and puts a pressure from within which breaks the skin as soon as the pressure of the water is relieved by the insect having reached the surface. On these occasions no more activity would be necessary than just enough to enable the nymph to maintain its balance and to reach the surface with

---

[1] I found *one* (my first) in a 2¾ pounder caught in August 1938.

its back upwards so as to be the right way up for hatching.

I have already quoted from pages 233-235 of *Dry Fly Fishing in Theory and Practice* Halford's description of a mature nymph observed under a microscope which is at least not inconsistent with my suggestion.

Here Halford clearly distinguishes the mature nymph from the immature—the mature showing the complete subimago floating and enveloped in what he describes as an apparently loose covering.

Now this covering includes the eyes of the nymph; and Halford shows that this covering is shed in the act of hatching. It did not seem to me an unwarrantable deduction to infer that when the nymph is ascending to hatch out with its eye-coverings and its breathing apparatus on the verge of detachment it will not for the moment have a degree of eyesight and power of movement such as would enable the active immature nymph to make some effort to escape.

When therefore we find (as we do find) the trout lined up under banks and meeting and taking the mature nymph close to the surface quietly and systematically without haste or pursuit, I think we are entitled to infer that the mature nymphs they are taking are, for the moment, practically inert to the extent at any rate of being powerless to resist the current or to make any effort to escape.

In confirmation of this view I may mention that I have watched by the hour the mature nymphs of the Mayfly coming up to hatch and they seemed entirely helpless as they were carried down-stream, neither wriggling nor making any effort to control their progress nor indeed showing any activity until, as they reached the surface, the shucks split down the back and the subimagines started to draw themselves free of them.

So far I have been setting out the conclusions at which

THE WAY OF A TROUT WITH A NYMPH

I had arrived as a result of my personal observations. I do not wish however to be less than entirely candid with my readers—so I feel bound to say that my views as to the inertness of the nymph about to hatch have been challenged by a dry-fly purist on no less an authority than that of my old and good friend, Martin E. Mosely. I therefore wrote to him on the subject, and with his authority I am setting out here verbatim the terms of his reply:

With regard to your question about nymphs: the mode of progress of the ephemerid nymph is by a series of extremely violent undulations of the abdomen which last for a few seconds. This seems to exhaust the insect so that its exertions are followed by a period of a few seconds inertia. When it is thus rested the rapid motion recommences and so on, until it reaches the surface. Here its arrival may coincide with a period of activity or inertness—it's a toss up. But when in the act of emerging the nymph is inert it is not beneath but *on* the surface with the thorax above water, probably at a higher level than that of the spent spinner.

It is incorrect to suppose that the nymph is borne up to the surface by gas. It swims up.

In reply to a further question he added later:

I have personally watched the ephemerid nymphs not only by the river side, but also in my aquarium where I have kept continued observation of nymphs up to and including their emergence on the surface.

This is more than I have had means or opportunity of doing. But his statement as to the activity of the ephemerid nymph does credit it with periods of inertia—and my thirty years' experience of taking good trout with artificial nymphs shows me conclusively that the periods of inertia at and near the surface are sufficiently common to cause trout to line up under banks and in rivers where they may meet and capture the inert nymph with a minimum of trouble. The reason for my insistence on the inertia of the mature nymph is that

Halford's reason for saying that the trout will not look at the artificial nymph is because of the activity of the natural nymph as contrasted with the deadness of the artificial. There must therefore be many occasions when the natural nymph is so inert as to be well represented by the artificial, since I have for years been finding Halford radically wrong in saying that the trout will not look at the artificial.

This question is debated more at large in the chapter on Halford's pronouncements.

On the question whether the nymph is helped to the surface by distension, whether by gas or otherwise, while giving every weight to Mosely's unique authority I would ask how in the moment of emergence the nymph is *on* the surface with the thorax above water unless there is some distension which, without altering the insect's total weight, reduces its specific gravity and assists flotation. Nothing in nature happens without reason and if the reason in this case be not distension I would respectfully ask what else it can be.

V

RODS AND GEAR

INASMUCH as nymph fishing is only one phase of chalkstream fishing and can only be pursued with success when the trout are nymphing, and as there are many occasions when the floating fly is the obvious and proper method to use, it is an advantage for the nymph fisher that the rod and line suitable for nymph fishing are suitable for fishing the dry fly. Conversely by no means every rod and line suitable for dry-fly fishing is suitable for fishing the nymph.

To the end of his days the rods and lines used and recommended by Halford for dry-fly fishing were quite unsuited to the delivery to a sitting trout of a nymph or wet fly, so that it would sink immediately on reaching the surface. The stiff rod driving a heavy line through the air was well devised to dry off every particle of moisture from the cast and the fly before the latter reached the fish. The appropriate type of rod for nymph fishing is easy enough in its action to deliver the nymph lightly and accurately, with the main part of the gut cast dry enough to float (oiled, if necessary, for the purpose) but with the nymph still retaining enough of the moisture to sink and carry with it the last two or three feet of fine gut, before it drifts over the trout to which it is cast. The line must not of course be propelled backwards and forwards through the air as it is being let out to reach the trout, but nymph and gut at each forward throw must be allowed to reach and enter the water, so that the nymph and the point are kept wet and sink on alighting above the fish. The line, to be suitable for fishing dry fly, wet fly or nymph, according to the conditions of the moment, must be heavy enough to cast when requisite into a moderate wind and to take its part in drying a fly—but not so heavy as to dry the cast too readily.

Assuming the angler to be provided with suitable rod, line and landing-net together with a selection of appropriately dressed nymph patterns and gut casts tapered to 3X or 4X, he is sufficiently equipped for nymph fishing but for one thing. He would be well advised to provide himself with a marrow scoop (see illustration, p. 16) in order to extract the contents of his trouts' stomachs and a metal cup with white-enamel lining into which to wash these contents from the scoop for inspection. For the capture of his first trout he must rely on his judgment of what is being taken, basing his estimate on the type of natural fly which he sees in the air or floating down on the water, or failing that, on one or other of the species in season. Thus he will probably be able to make a pretty good guess and he may hope, with perhaps one or two changes of pattern, to get a trout fairly soon. But having got him and knocked him on the head, he can bring the marrow scoop into play, wetting it, passing it down into the trout's belly and with one twist bringing up the entire contents practically uninjured. These, washed out into the metal cup, should show him exactly what his trout has been taking, and he may select the most likely representation of it from his stock of nymph patterns. The marrow scoop may, if he be a fly dresser, be again brought into play on his return home, to bring out the contents of all his fish and to float them in a suitable dish with a white china bottom, where they can be under his inspection while he dresses representations of an exactitude otherwise difficult if not impossible.

Though the marrow scoop is here recommended for chalk-stream fishing it would no doubt be of even greater real service to anglers on other streams and of some service to the dry-fly man on every stream.

VI

FISHING THE NYMPH

NYMPH fishing on chalk streams is not, like wet-fly fishing on rough streams, an exclusive or a practically exclusive method. It is a form of trout fishing on chalk streams to be practised only where the behaviour of the trout demands it, just as fishing the floating fly is to be practised where the behaviour of the trout demands it, the two forms providing together a far more comprehensive equipment for the angler than either alone.

But whether the angler be a purist confining himself to the floating fly or a practitioner of both methods as occasion may require, it is equally necessary that he should make such a study of the feeding habits of the fish as will enable him to judge which of the two methods is appropriate to the conditions of the moment, so that he may not be presenting nymphs to a fish which is feeding on super-surface food or pestering with floating patterns fish which are for the time being confining themselves to subaqueous food while letting the floating natural insect go by.

I think it well therefore that I should deal as comprehensively as my experience and equipment will permit me with those indications which the rise-forms made by trout taking insect food of various kinds and in varying conditions present to the angler, as affording clues as to what they are feeding on and how and where.

In an article published in the *Fly Fishers' Club Journal* under the title "Assorted Rises" and republished in 1921 in a chapter, also so headed, in *The Way of a Trout with a Fly*, I made what was, I believe, the first serious attempt to help the fly fisher to distinguish from the character of the rise what it is on which the trout is for the time being feeding, and how and where.

In 1925, in *Divers Ways to tackle Trout*, and later in 1929 in *Trout Fishing from All Angles*, Eric Taverner made, under the much happier title "Rise Forms", more extended and detailed examinations of the same phenomena, without however substantially challenging the general basis of the analysis in "Assorted Rises".

As however it is my aim to make this volume comprehensive on its subject I will not refer my readers either to Eric Taverner's work or my own, but I will endeavour to summarise, as clearly and precisely as I can, the conclusions which have so far been reached, but I should like to emphasise here what I pointed out in "Assorted Rises," namely that where the food insect is found by the fish in conditions which render it helpless and unable to make any effort to escape, as in the case of an inert hatching nymph, the trout takes with a gentleness and absence of flurry far different from his action in taking an insect capable of effort to escape.

The insect food of trout (apart from caterpillars, moths, crane-flies, cow-dung and other land flies and ants which wind or rain or accident may precipitate upon the water) comprises:

(1) Ephemeridae in their successive larval and nymphal stages and in their winged stages as duns or Sub-imagines or as Imagines or Spinners both living and spent, or in some cases crawling under water to lay their eggs.

(2) Phryganidae or Sedge or Caddis flies in the under-

water stages when they inhabit cases and crawl on the bottom—stages in which they are of no use to the fly fisher—in the stage in which, leaving the shelter of their cases, they find their way to the surface to hatch out with great suddenness as winged flies and are apt to be attacked by the trout while on their way up—a phase which is seldom of much use to the fly fisher as the hatch is never (except perhaps in the case of a copious hatch of grannom) sufficiently concentrated in one place or line of places to enable the angler by their means to find a trout in position—and in the winged stage when they run on the surface or dance over it in the business of oviposition.

(3) Perlidae or Stone flies which are not so common on chalk streams as to provide a regular article of diet and are only of use to the angler occasionally—and that not in their under-water or creeper stage, though the representation of the hatched Willow fly in autumn is often best taken as a sunk fly.

(4) The Alder, which passes its preliminary active stages in the river mud, then crawls ashore to bury itself in the earth for its pupal period and eventually hatches out as a terrestrial fly, seldom seen on the water and even then, on some rivers like the Itchen, seldom taken on the surface—while on other rivers such as the Kennet, the artificial representation well sunk is deadly.

(5) Gnats in their under-water stages, both larval and pupal and in their winged stage.

(6) Smuts.

(7) Water beetles, some of which are subaqueous and others skitter about on the surface, being taken by the trout with a slash.

So far as these insects are taken on the surface they are matters of dry-fly fishing. So far as they are taken subaqueously they are matters of ordinary wet-fly fishing, but only the larval stages of the Ephemeridae are represented in nymph fishing. Fortunately on most chalk streams the nymphs of the Ephemeridae constitute the main diet of the trout at such periods as they are feeding at or near the surface. Wet-fly fishing was practised in chalk streams for generations before the dry fly came (and no doubt a proportion of the wet flies presented to the trout were taken for nymphs), but the deliberate practice of seeking to take the trout with a close representation, in size, colour, bulk and outline, of the nymph on which he is for the moment feeding is an innovation of the present century, and still very much misunderstood if one may judge from the monstrosities and absurdities offered and sold by so many of the tackle dealers as nymphs and accepted as such by anglers.

It therefore behoves the angler who would take the best advantage of the new method to watch the behaviour of feeding trout closely, so that he may be able to judge whether feeding fish are in fact nymphing or surface-feeding or are taking subaqueously some other food than nymphs.

In nymph fishing the artificial nymph has to be presented with the maximum of precision to selected individual feeding fish in position, and it should be cast either directly up-stream, up-stream and across, or directly across, or, on occasions even slightly down, with such gentleness and delicacy as to ensure that, without scaring the fish, the artificial nymph and an adequate part of the gut cast shall have sunk before the nymph reaches the fish, but not far enough above him to drag until it is past him.

FISHING THE NYMPH

The angler should be at pains to study the rise-forms which he finds the trout making and to confine his attention to those which indicate really sizable fish; there need be no occasion for the hooking, injuring and returning of trout too small to be kept. I myself am in favour of a number limit and the return of no caught fish to the water. There is no better method of ensuring that the angler shall leave the small trout alone and devote his attention to those really worth keeping according to the standard of the water, and that too whether his method of fishing be dry or wet or either according to the conditions of the moment.

Apart from having one's artificial nymphs constructed of materials which readily take up water there are several methods of assisting them to sink. The simplest and most obvious is the use of saliva, both on the nymph and on the bottom couple of lengths of the gut cast. That is a process which, especially on a hot dry day, may require frequent renewal. Another method is to apply a little glycerine to the same parts; a third is to anoint the same length of gut or the nymph with a little river mud or with moist clay. Each of these processes may require renewal from time to time. These observations apply equally whether the trout cast to be tailing, bulging or taking the natural nymph quietly near the surface without pursuit on the trout's part or effort to escape on the part of the nymph.

The opportunities afforded by tailing fish are few. Those afforded by bulging trout are more frequent, but still only occasional. I have already described what is meant by "bulging". It is hard to say what are the conditions which cause the trout to bulge. A fit of bulging is often accompanied by a relatively tiny hatch of fly, and it may be that the nymphs, for some obscure motive (perhaps migration to another pasture), come out of their fastnesses for a spell and return (in greatly reduced numbers) to their fastnesses in the same or another bed of weeds.

Fishing with nymph to bulging fish, unless one casts to them up-stream or up and across, is much more apt to lead to fishing down with a dragging fly than any other form of nymph fishing. Indeed that method was expressly recommended by Dr J. C. Mottram in his *Fly Fishing: Some New Arts and Mysteries*. And it may be that a revulsion from such methods (I cannot commend them) has of late driven Dr Mottram back into the ranks of the dry-fly purists. The dragging method *is*, of course, apt to lead to the hooking and mishandling of undersized fish, and is therefore rightly objected to.

The drawback in casting to bulging trout, whether with dry fly, wet fly or nymph, is that the place where the bulge last occurred is almost invariably the place where the trout is *not* a moment later, and I have already deprecated the method of getting over this difficulty by casting a dragging wet fly or nymph across the weed-bed where bulging trout are feeding. Bulging trout are not easily scared by being cast over, and anyhow an up-stream cast can be withdrawn, if it fails, without any disturbance of the water; and the sway of the weeds may impart enough motion to the natural nymph to attract the trout.

The type of nymph to be offered to bulgers may be the same as might at the same season be offered to a trout quietly nymphing under a bank, but one of the Tup's Indispensable type specially dressed to sink is often very effective.

Beyond question therefore the angler's best chance with a nymphing fish is with one which is taking nymph quietly and without haste or pursuit either under a bank or in a run or at the tail of a good nymph-holding type of weed.

FISHING THE NYMPH

Such trout do not move about much, often continue nymphing for a considerable time, and thus can be cast to with greater precision than any others.

In this condition it is obvious that for the artificial nymph to approach the trout like a natural mature nymph it must be fished so as to reach the trout without drag, for, as I have shown, the mature natural nymph, being inert, must come to the fish with the current and without drag.

Occasionally one may see quite good trout in the middle of a strong stream, seldom breaking the surface, but moving slightly to and fro, pale *café-au-lait* coloured shadows intercepting under water the natural nymphs coming down in the strength of the current. These are usually lusty and powerful fish.

When trout are feeding steadily under water and are letting the winged fly go over them unmarked it is usually because there is a strong and steady stream of nymphs being brought to them by the current. And so long as that stream of nymphs offers steadier and more profitable feeding than the floating dun so long will the trout continue to take the nymph and let the fly go by. I have however observed occasions when the wind, driving the hatched-out flies under one bank, has so concentrated them that the stream of hatched-out flies outnumber the nymphs and the trout soon begin to take the floating fly. I have indeed on more than one occasion found trout nymphing under one length of bank and neglecting the hatched-out fly, while just round a bend where the wind concentrated the hatched fly under the bank the fish were busy with them there.

Where however the hatch has practically ceased, any trout which remains in position has his attention no longer concentrated on a stream of nymphs or flies, and, if still unsatisfied and rising, is sometimes ready to take whichever comes along, and this is why a casual feeder who goes on after the main hatch is over is generally a comparatively easy fish. A small Red Sedge, a Pheasant Tail, a Tup's Indispensable, floating to represent a spinner or sunk to represent a nymph, may equally well do his business, for he has no longer a stream of natural insects with which to compare them. I have latterly wondered at times whether the explanation of the trout taking under-water winged wet flies that in shape do not resemble nymphs but upwinged duns or sedges, may not be that they see approaching them not only the artificial sunk fly but also its reflection in the mirror which the underside of the surface film provides outside the trout's window. The fish thus sees two forms approaching him, one, the real, under water, and the other, the reflection, just as he sees the nymph, and feels that he must take the subaqueous fly in the same way as he takes the nymph. It seems a thin explanation, reflecting little credit on the trout's intelligence—but I have been unable to think of a better.

When trout and/or grayling are seen rising at something invisible and perhaps not quite breaking the surface, while letting upwinged duns go by, it is often difficult to judge whether they are taking nymphs or spent spinners. In each case they suck in something that is not an insect floating above the surface, but is either a spinner floating spent, and perhaps semi-submerged, a midge or a nymph just arriving at the surface and about to hatch out into a dun. When the rise is taking place under the angler's own bank, it is often possible to find out the fact by watching and observing what food the current brings. But when the rise is in the middle or under the far bank the problem is not so easy.

The late Colonel E. W. Harding in his invaluable volume,

FISHING THE NYMPH

The Flyfisher and the Trout's Point of View, shows how the trout lying in wait with an upward gaze below a smooth surface is enabled to watch the reflection of the approaching nymph in the mirror made by the surface beyond the window through which he can see—and how, in order to keep the reflection in view of his upward gaze, he has to come up to the surface to meet the actual nymph as it and its reflection come together there. Thus his rise to a nymph under such conditions and to a spent spinner both culminate at the surface and bear a close resemblance to one another, a resemblance accentuated by the fact that neither inert nymph nor spent spinner can make any effort to escape.

There are however clues which may be of assistance to the angler in determining whether the quarry be spent spinner or nymph. Upwinged duns and spinners that are not spent are generally driven by the wind, even if it be no more than a light air, under one bank or another. Spent spinners however fall all over the water and go down spent where they fall instead of being wind-driven under either bank; and often where there is a heavy spinner fall in the middle of the river trout will be roaming in mid-stream to meet them. This is particularly noticeable of an evening, when trout rising under either bank may in general be suspected of feeding either on duns or nymphs. In places however where the strength of the stream is in the middle the trout may still be taking nymphs and not spinners, and it is difficult to tell which. Where however one finds trout rising to something invisible below collections of weed either growing from the bottom and rising above the surface or cut and collected against the bank, so that the surface of the current is obstructed and neither upwinged dun nor spinner can be brought to the fish, the inference that the trout is taking nymphs is irresistible.

NYMPH FISHING FOR CHALK STREAM TROUT

I had instances of these conditions recently on the Itchen. On the first occasion, late in June, a trout was rising steadily but infrequently under the far bank in quite smooth water behind a patch of weeds floating on the surface where it was impossible for any upwinged dun or any spinner, living or spent, to reach him. The conclusion therefore was that he must be taking nymphs emerging from the weed bed and about to hatch. The trout took my artificial nymph the first time it reached him, and proved to be $2\frac{1}{4}$ lb.—a good fish for the Itchen.

On the second occasion the trout was rising under similar conditions behind a patch of cut weed lodged on a bed of weed under the far bank, and, taking my nymph at the first offer, proved to be 3 lb. 14 oz. Both of these fish had only nymphs in their crops. They are instances also to show how mistaken Halford was in his pronouncement that the wet fly was useless in conditions of bright sun and smooth surface, and that only small fish can be caught with it.

Another pointer for the angler is the rate at which the trout is taking. If he be rising frequently, it is much easier to judge whether he be taking nymph or spent spinner—whether he be rising under a bank or out in the open stream, unless the weather be quite still and a heavy fall of spent spinner has been observed. In that case spinner may be inferred.

In some conditions of light it is possible to detect trout lying under a further bank, not breaking the surface at all since the rise has not got into full swing but obviously lying in wait. Then an appropriate nymph dropped a yard or so above them will often bring them out a few inches, and if one tightens as the trout's head turns back to the bank the hook is usually found to have gone home.

When a fish is rising in mid-stream and cruising, he may

FISHING THE NYMPH

be taking spent spinner or nymph, but a rise to spent spinner is often distinguished by a head and tail action, elsewhere described as "the porpoise roll". But here again the frequency or infrequency of the rise may afford a useful indication of what the trout is really doing. Nymphs in a strong current are generally more frequent than spent spinners and are moreover more readily perceived by the trout even at a little distance and a proportion of them are taken well below the surface.

I have already pointed out that in presenting an artificial nymph to a trout in position it is essential that not only should it sink on alighting, but that it should draw with it two feet or more of the cast, otherwise a fatal drag may occur. The nymph should be dressed with a short soft hackle and of material to take up water and the line should not be dried by successive casts in the air—but at each cast in letting out line to reach the fish the nymph and gut should come down on the water so that in the final cast which reaches the trout the last two feet or more of the gut shall be wet. If the wind will serve across stream a switch cast may well be adopted and in subsequent casts the manœuvre known as "picking it off" (p. 183 of *The Way of a Trout*) enables the nymph to be delivered in the right state of moisture. This operation is carried out as follows: Assuming that you are on the right bank of the stream with the flow from left to right and that you have laid your cast across and desire to pick it up for a fresh cast. You move your rod-top briskly out to the right and then up and round in a rapid forward curve to the left. This picks up the heaviest part of the line and, bellying it in a long single curve, lifts it into the air, leaving little but the gut on the water, whence it should be picked off for the back cast before any part of the line has time to fall back into the water. This puts the minimum of strain on the rod, and in the forward cast the nymph and the fine end of the gut are delivered with the least possible amount of drying to the fish. The method can easily be learnt. The part of the gut intended to float may be greased or oiled.

I am not suggesting that it is only at the surface that trout take the inert nymphs on their way up to hatch, for every now and then a deeper swirl or a mere hump on the water tells one that a trout has met and absorbed a nymph at a lower level. And indeed, were it otherwise, it would be a poor look-out for the nymph angler, for most of his fish must take his artificial nymph below the surface, from 1 inch or less to perhaps 5 or 6 inches. The shape, size and energy of the rise form do however give the nymph angler useful means of judging whether the riser be a sizable or big fish or one which it is his business, as a good sportsman, to avoid. A nymphing fish should not, any more than should a trout taking the floating natural fly, be cast to until the angler has fairly judged him to be at least sizable according to the standard of the water. If care be taken in this respect the angler is no more likely to hook unsizable fish with nymph than with a floating fly.

Though in general the angler will find his best profit in presenting his artificial nymph as if it were a natural nymph on its way to hatch, yet there are occasions when the trout may be found taking the active nymph. Of these occasions the more important occurs after weed cutting when the growing nymph, feeling the vegetation which was his habitat no longer fixed to the soil, but cut adrift, is apt to seek temporary refuge out of the current in little bays under the bank. Here the trout finds him out, and here at times an artificial nymph of appropriate size and colour cast into the bay, and dragged out by the force of the current on the

FISHING THE NYMPH

line, is apt to attract the attention of the trout and to be followed and taken with a plunge. Trout taken thus are generally big. I recall an occasion when from the far bank I saw four trout busy in such a tiny backwater about a yard wide, and, offering a nymph, I succeeded in hooking all four of them in succession and landing three.

Sometimes it will happen that an artificial nymph sent to a trout rising quietly under the bank or in a run will be taken so close to the surface and as obviously as a dry fly would be. Sometimes the trout may even be seen to turn at the nymph. Then there is no difficulty about striking. But oftener the signs of a trout's acceptance of the nymph are far subtler and less obvious and may at times be so slight that the angler who has responded to one or other of them and hooked his trout may be unable to say precisely why he struck. The more obvious signs may be described as follows:

The first I may call "the draw" which may occur in several different conditions according to whether the nymph has been delivered in fast water or in slow, directly upstream or up and across, directly across or across and slightly down. The feature of the draw is the sudden acceleration of the pace of sinking of the fine end of the cast with its attached nymph. The response to this signal must be immediate or the fish will be gone.

Too frequently however conditions of light prevent the angler from detecting the draw. He may however sometimes discern some subtle shift of colour or movement of the water caused by the fish turning to take the nymph.

At times when, casting directly up-stream over deepish water one detects a dim fawn-coloured shadow busy intercepting nymphs and seldom breaking the surface, then even if one does not see the draw one may infer the taking by observing the fawn brown shadow move to the spot where one infers one's nymph to be and then turn back into the straight—and then the response may be rewarded by a tight line. But even if it be not, the recovery of line and nymph under water is less apt to alarm the feeding fish than would a futile strike at a rise to a floating fly.

Sometimes the taking will be indicated by a slight humping of the surface looking like a soup plate upside down with a pinhole in the middle or a crinkle coming to the surface. Practice and close attention may in time develop in the chalk stream nymph-fisher a sort of instinct akin to that of the first-rate up-stream wet-fly fisher on rough rivers. The latter however have the advantage, not available to the chalk stream angler, of fishing with a tight line, so that he is always in touch with his fly—with the result that a taking trout is apt to hook himself.

Sometimes a fish will be found nymphing in mid-stream. This may take place in a run where the trout feeds in position, much as he does under a bank, and he must generally be fished to up and more or less across. Or he may be cruising over a greater or less area of open flat water. If he can be seen he can be cast to with a fair chance of success provided the angler keep low. If however, as is generally the case, he cannot be seen, the chances of lining him or putting him down are greatly increased, and it is seldom of any use to cast to a cruiser at the place of the last rise, as he has almost always moved on. The most frequent case of cruising trout taking nymphs is of an evening during a strong rise of the blue-winged olive.

A strong adverse breeze into which the nymph and gut cast have to be forced is inimical to nymph-fishing, because the force used in casting into it tends to dry both gut and nymph—and drag may result from the gut and nymph as

FISHING THE NYMPH

fatal to the capture of the trout as the drag of a fully floating fly. Such a breeze moreover generally creates a ruffle which prevents the fish from seeing the approaching nymph reflected in the surface mirror. It will as a rule be found therefore that a ruffle due to breeze, whether adverse or not, is not conducive to trout in position taking the nymph under the ruffled surface so as to be detected by the angler. When in such circumstances trout are found nymphing it is more frequently than not in smooth unruffled water; and if the fish can be approached with the wind, whether from directly below, or across and up, straight across, or across and slightly down, the nymph can best be delivered so as to sink immediately and to reach the fish in the best position to be taken.

It should be noted that a nymph cast directly up-stream is apt to sink more rapidly than one cast across. It is best therefore in such conditions not to cast too far above the trout and to let the line fall to the left or right of him rather than directly over. The nearer one's nymph is to the surface the easier it is to detect the rise, while a cast not too far to one side or the other of him may bring the fish across to the nymph, perhaps in sight of the angler, and is less likely to line the trout than one made directly over him. The direction of the light too should be watched and the nymph preferably placed to the side in shade of the bank. These considerations also apply to a casting across stream.

If the nymph be cast directly up-stream, drag is not much to be feared, but if across care should be taken so to handle the line that the nymph does not begin to drag out until it has passed the trout. Here the reader will realise why I have been elsewhere so insistent on the inertness of the natural nymph on its way to hatch. It may be that where a lure-type of so-called nymph is used, it is more effective dragging than following the course of the current. But where the nymph pattern is a good representation of the natural insect it is more likely to be taken if it follows the course of the natural nymph and is brought down in the same line by the current. It would follow as a matter of course that, if not allowed to drag till it is past the fish, a nymph cast across, even if slightly down, is less likely to alarm the trout by lining him than if cast straight up-stream to him. A nymph approaching has not to be seen by the fish through his window, but can be seen either by reflection in the mirror or by direct vision even a yard or so away, and if it be the right pattern and attractive the trout is not unlikely to sail over to it and take it. Sometimes the entire operation can be seen by the angler, and a strike, delivered as the fish turns back to resume his post, results in a firmly hooked trout.

I deal elsewhere with the type of pattern which most fairly represents the natural nymph. I am as firmly set against the use of fancy patterns and lures under the name of nymphs as was Halford in his later days against fancy floating flies, and I strongly urge the use of the best representation which the angler can dress or procure, resembling, when wet, the natural nymph in size, colour and form.

It may be noted that the most favourable conditions for finding trout feeding quietly on the rising nymph are where the current sets strongly under the bank and the surface is unruffled, for in these conditions trout can make best use of the surface mirror.

Where, on the other hand, the surface is ruffled, particularly by wind, the surface of the mirror is broken and obscured and trout must either be reduced to meeting the nymph well below the surface or seeking his prey elsewhere.

This reasoning no doubt accounts for the fact, which in

FISHING THE NYMPH

my youth puzzled me sorely, that in rough North Country and Scottish streams it is the rarest thing to see the surface broken by a rising trout. The mirror in these cases is almost, if not entirely, useless to the fish, which must therefore catch his prey in mid-water. In such waters "the time of the take", as it is called, depends on the hour when the nymph is on its way to hatch, but the rough-water angler is in general deprived of the evidence of the break of the surface which tells the smooth-water angler not only where to find the fish but when it is on the feed.

The rough-stream angler therefore has to fish with a line so tight as to render it probable that a taking trout will hook himself and the broken nature of the current no doubt accustoms the fish to all sorts of vagaries of drag.

Both the spent spinner and the nymph taken in a "dimpling" rise are absorbed with a definite suck. The head and tail rise or porpoise roll in general suggest spinner, though I have known occasions when the nymph has been taken with a head and tail rise, particularly in quiet bays out of the current. This always seems to me to indicate that the fish are quietly taking something which has little or no chance of escape, into the air or otherwise. Anyhow, it sometimes makes it very difficult for the angler to determine what the particular quarry is. Spinner-fall often precedes the general rise in the morning. Later on in the morning and through the day the sucking rise suggests nymph. But in the early evening, especially when it occurs in midstream, spinner is generally, but not always, a better bet than nymph.

I do want to insist again, as I did concerning the wet fly in *Minor Tactics of the Chalk Stream*, that I am firmly against fishing the water in any form—and I agree fully with those who claim that that kind of practice and fishing a dragging fly down-stream *is* detrimental, that it leads to hooking or injuring or pricking and searing unsizable fish, and that the only legitimate method of nymph fishing and the true sporting method is to cast to the individual selected subaqueously feeding fish.

Mayfly Nymphs

The Mayfly has long ceased to exist on my length of the Itchen and it is long since I fished Mayfly anywhere. But on those occasions when I found trout taking the Mayfly nymph they seemed to snatch it, as if afraid of it, and to dash off with such speed that, by the time the boil of their turn reached the surface, they were yards away. In fact they were bulging. I never saw them taking Mayfly nymphs at the surface calmly and gently as they take the nymphs of the smaller Ephemeridae. So far as I know therefore the methods of nymph fishing applicable to the smaller Ephemeridae are not suitable to fishing the nymph of the Mayfly. The only occasion when I have heard anything to the contrary was when a friend of mine, an excellent angler, visited during the Mayfly season a big house on the Kennet as one of a week-end party of four or five, and having dressed some imitations of the Mayfly nymph, took with them during his stay, not only more trout than any other member of the party, but more daily and in the aggregate than all the others put together. But I do not know how he fished his artificial nymph.

VII

EXCEPTIONS

I DO not wish to be less than entirely candid with my readers and I therefore feel bound to mention that there are three upwinged floating fly patterns which will on occasion attract a nymph-taking trout to the surface.

The first is the Gold-ribbed Hare's Ear, a pattern extolled by F. M. Halford in his earlier books and later on abandoned. He claimed that it would take trout throughout the season. My own experience is that it is specially successful in the season of the large Medium Olive Dun of spring. There is little doubt that this pattern must be taken for a hatching nymph standing on its partially discarded shuck. Indeed this was substantially Halford's own opinion.

Another gold-ribbed pattern which I have found specially attractive to tailing trout (which are of course often nymphing) is Pope's Green Nondescript—the invention of Mr W. H. Pope—which the late George Holland used to dress beautifully and correctly, but which is now practically unobtainable, as none of the dressers seem to use the right coloured bright but palish-green floss for the body.

The third is the Red Quill with a ribbed body of stripped *undyed* peacock herl and a sharp, bright red cock's hackle. The reason why this is occasionally taken by nymphing fish I have never been able to fathom.

Apart from these three patterns I know of none which attract the nymphing trout. I have long discarded both

Wickham's Fancy and the Pink Wickham, with the latter of which I had some success with tailing trout.

The Gold-ribbed Hare's Ear appears to me to be a fair fly to use as it suggests something definite which the trout may be taking. The attraction of Pope's Green Nondescript I confess myself unable to explain—the Red Quill *may* be taken for a spinner which a trout taking nymphs as they arrive at the surface might be occasionally tempted to accept—but this is a mere guess.

It is observable that where the water runs fast, as in places where it is let out through a hatch to irrigate meadows, though the fish are no doubt taking their quota of nymphs, they are far more amenable to the attraction of a floating fly such as a Red Sedge on a No. 2 hook or a seal's fur-bodied claret spinner of similar size than in the more regular flow of the main stream—and this is probably to some extent true of the main stream where it is shallow and flows fast with a broken surface over and between weeds.

VIII

PERSONAL

THE history of my personal connection with the subject of this volume has been one of slow development.

After a couple of ineffective seasons (1875-1876) on the Old Barge river at Winchester while a boy at the school, with an impossible rod and line and with flies supposed to be fished dry but in build best suited to be fished downstream wet, and some odd days on the Thames and Colne with dace and chub, and on the Tweed and South Esk with trout, I had the fortune in 1883 to be invited by the late Irwin E. B. Cox (then one of the proprietors of the *Field*) to fish the length of the Itchen he had recently rented, and there I met Francis Francis, who was then Angling Editor of the *Field*, and William Senior who succeeded him. The beautifully tied split-winged floaters which I saw at the Fisheries Exhibition of that year, so much better than the flies I had hitherto used, and the charm of the Itchen with its store of free-rising trout, and the success of Francis Francis in taking a leash of 2-pounders on my first day, inspired in me an enthusiasm for the floating fly which was clinched when, in 1887, I was presented with Halford's *Floating Flies and how to Dress Them*. In the latter part of that year I took up trout-fly dressing with enthusiasm and I read in the British Museum and elsewhere every book I could find on the subject and analysed and recorded the dressings.

My days on the Itchen became yearly more frequent, and

NYMPH FISHING FOR CHALK STREAM TROUT

I had more wet-fly fishing on the Tweed and South Esk, and in 1888 I had a week or so on the Coquet in September. I recall that about that year I suggested to George Holland, the well-known professional fly dresser with whom I got into correspondence, that he should dress a trout fly with a piece of sponge for body material to make it sink. About the same time a friend gave me the 1883 edition of Cutcliffe's *Trout Fishing in Rapid Streams*. It was about then I got into correspondence through the *Fishing Gazette* with the late R. S. Austin—not realising for a long time that he was not an amateur.

In 1889 I became the happy owner of Halford's *Dry Fly Fishing in Theory and Practice* which became to me, as to many others, a sort of gospel.

Mr Cox continued to give me more and more days on the Itchen. From the first I was rising and hooking trout, but I foolishly used gossamer gut and I left an undue proportion of my flies in the fish in the strike. One Saturday I was fishing at a spot where a strong stream emerged from a hatch and I left my fly (a Pink Wickham) and two lengths of gut point in a fish. Next Monday, fishing at the same place with another Pink Wickham, I caught and killed the same fish with the fly in his mouth and half a yard or more of gut attached, and in recovering the fly I found his mouth was full of small bright green nymphs. This was my first observation of the kind and my first realisation that trout did not feed exclusively on the winged fly—though I had been struck by a mocking remark of a correspondent of the *Fishing Gazette* to the effect that anglers were foolish if they supposed that flies were what trout fed on. It looks as if he had not realised that the nymph was the fly in an earlier stage.

On Mr Cox's Itchen water I used to meet an old retired

PERSONAL

solicitor named Godwin who used a long soft rod 13 or 14 feet long and fished a wet fly with a good entry downstream, or across and down (just in fact the type of fly supplied to me as a boy by old John Hammond for use on the Old Barge length of the Itchen)—and he explained to me how trout were caught before the advent of the dry fly by fishing a wet fly down-stream over the tails of weed beds. But I did not realise, nor I believe did he, that his flies thus fished were taken for swimming nymphs.

There were, however, two nephews of Mr Cox who on rough days of down-stream wind would fish the Itchen down-stream with two or three biggish flies and caught big baskets, mainly of small trout, but as a disciple of Halford I felt no disposition to follow their example. I had meanwhile some further wet-fly experience on the Yore, and I grew more and more puzzled to understand why the dry fly should be exclusively used on chalk streams, when before its advent big baskets were caught with the wet fly.

In September 1891 I met F. M. Halford on the Abbots' Barton water and had a week's fishing with him; and in the evenings I used, with a number of others, to visit him in his room at the George Hotel and listen (with becoming reverence) to him while he held forth on the dry fly. Two years later, on the sponsorship of Halford and William Senior, I became a member of the Fly Fishers' Club and took a keen and active part in its doings.

Trout frequently bulged on the Itchen and I could not for the life of me see why they should be fished with dry flies when they were obviously feeding under water. I guessed from my wet-fly experience on other rivers that some flies such as were effective on the Tweed and elsewhere might be effective with Itchen bulger. So I began to experiment on the bulgers with small double-hooked

Greenwell's Glories such as Mr Ewen M. Tod recommended for his Scotch waters and with occasional success.

From that I took to trying the same pattern and later other wet flies on trout which, though rising in position under the banks, could not be seen to take floating sub-imagines, still being puzzled to discern the reason why trout took winged patterns under water—but more and more certain that there must be some good reason in nature for their doing so. In 1899 the *Field* published a letter from me in which I stated my conviction that anglers on chalk streams would have to go back to the wet fly on occasions where trout were not surface feeding. This letter was recalled to my memory by my late friend, H. T. Sheringham (then Angling Editor of the *Field*), a short time before his death, and it was reprinted for historical reasons at pages 59 and 60 of my third volume, *Side Lines, Side Lights and Reflections*.

I began to make an occasional autopsy, finding the fish generally full of nymph, with few winged flies or none, and I gradually extended my practice of using the wet fly on occasions when the dry fly failed or was obviously not being taken. I also had had in the 'nineties some dry-fly experience on the Derbyshire Derwent, Wye and Manifold, besides having several Mayfly seasons on the Lower Kennet where there were plenty of big chub and the few trout I caught averaged about 3 lb.

In 1899 I visited a limestone river in Bavaria, very like a chalk stream in character, and for a number of years thereafter up to 1909 I fished it pretty regularly—finding, to my surprise, that a large sunk Alder was very successful, and that small wet flies often did better than small floaters. This, however, was not the case with big sedges.

I am omitting reference to other rivers, including Norwegian and Bosnian streams, which had little or no bearing on my progress towards nymph fishing in chalk streams.

I had for several years carried on a lengthy correspondence on fly dressing and fly fishing with Mr R. S. Austin and in 1900 he communicated to me his discovery of the since famous trout-fly pattern to which I gave the name "Tup's Indispensable". I thought at first it was (as he intended it to be) merely a red spinner and as such I soon found it more successful semi-submerged than floating. Later I discovered that, dressed with less red seal's fur mixed in the dubbing, it was by no means a bad representation of one of the nymphs which looks as if it were bleeding at the thorax. It led to my dressing for myself and using a small range of nymphs, including one of the Blue-winged Olive for use in the day-time.

In the 'nineties too I became acquainted with and warmly attached to the late Louis Bouglé, and fished with him on two or three Normandy chalk streams and was strongly encouraged by him to pursue my enquiries and experiments in the use of the wet fly on clear weedy rivers.

In 1902, being greatly impressed with the powers and quality of the American light trout fly rod, particularly the Leonard make, I flung myself actively into the controversy on the subject which raged in the angling press. The part which I took led to my making the acquaintance of the late Walter Durfee Coggeshall—an American long resident in London—and to my acquisition in 1903 of my first Leonard, a 10-footer. In 1905 a client presented me with "the best fly-rod money could buy", to be chosen by myself—and having been immensely struck by the quality of a 9-foot Leonard brought over in 1904 for the Crystal Palace Fly Casting Tournament by young Mr Mills of New York (whose firm built and sold the Leonard rods), I selected a duplicate which is still, after thirty-three years' hard wear, the joy of my life. It formed a strong contrast to the stiff and heavy weaver's beams which were the dry-fly rods in fashion in that day. It enabled me to cast a fly to sink on alighting, and I have no doubt it had a great effect in helping me with my experiments in wet-fly fishing with fly and nymph to individual trout in chalk streams. I discarded my Perfection 10-footer, my 11-foot Test Rod and another wrist-breaker.

By the end of 1909 the late H. T. Sheringham induced me to throw together a series of articles which I had contributed to the *Field*, the *Fishing Gazette* and the *Fly Fishers' Club Journal*, and to add some matter to link them up. The collection was illustrated by a number of my wet-fly patterns, including Tup's Indispensable and one olive nymph. It was called *Minor Tactics of the Chalk Stream*, and, advocating as it did the use of wet flies when trout were not taking floaters, it produced a certain sensation in the angling world. But though I believe I was regarded by some of the ultra dry-fly group as an exceedingly wicked man—a veritable lost soul —the storm of controversy which I had anticipated never materialised and the argument implicit in my volume evoked no solitary attempt to answer it. Still I was profoundly dissatisfied with my failure to account for trout taking the winged fly under water—a point on which my friend Bouglé commented with kindly humour.

In the next ten years or so I continued assiduously to practise the use of wet fly and nymph for trout which were neglecting the floating natural fly, and I contributed to the *Field* and the *Fly Fishers' Club Journal* during that period a number of articles, in which I discussed the eyesight of the trout and his other faculties and, collaterally, a number of papers of a type similar to those contained in *Minor*

Tactics of the Chalk Stream; and these were collected and published in 1921 under the title, *The Way of a Trout with a Fly*. This volume contained a description of two new methods of imitating the nymph more precisely than that illustrated in my previous volume.

Still I was not satisfied; and, having borrowed the family marrow scoop, I found it capable of extracting, with a single twist, the entire contents of the stomach of a trout. Soon afterwards I supplanted the cup or saucer into which I had washed out the contents of the marrow scoop by one of those heavy china plates with a strong incurved rim, made to prevent babies from spooning their food over the edge of the plate. And I found that in such a baby plate I could have the entire contents of a trout's stomach floating before me so that I could simulate the nymphs not only as to colour but as to length, taper, thickness and other detail with a precision previously impossible—and all this without any of the nauseating mess of an autopsy. So I set to work dressing a series of nymphs and testing them again and again on the trout, and with such success that I felt fully justified in having thrown off the shackles of the exclusive dry-fly doctrines of Halford and his school and in continuing to practise the presentation to feeding trout of wet fly and nymph, especially the nymph, *when they were feeding below the surface*. In the old days of the dry fly a 2-pounder was a rarity—I now began to get them fairly frequently and even an occasional 3-pounder.

Latterly too I found an increasing disposition on the part of chalk stream anglers to regard the use of the artificial nymph when trout were nymphing as a valuable addition to their technique—but at the same time a lamentable inability on the part of most tackle dealers to supply patterns having a real resemblance to any natural nymph. And I was assured not long ago by a distinguished Test angler that the Test was being fished with nymphs from Overton to the sea.

In another part of this volume I examine the teachings and claims of Halford and endeavour to show where he went wrong, and how but for some ineffective observation on his part he might have been of my opinion and have preached a very different doctrine.

I have turned back to *Minor Tactics of the Chalk Stream* (1910) and to *The Way of a Trout with a Fly* (1921) to verify my recollections of my earlier experiments with nymphs—and I find from the latter (published in 1921 but mainly written earlier), p. 123, that I had used imitations of nymphs on chalk streams for some fifteen seasons, and later in the same page I wrote:

> I can cordially concur in the oft-expressed wish that some wet-fly enthusiast would set to work and make exact reproductions of nymphs and larvae in the same way as Mr F. M. Halford treated the floating fly. And these should be submitted to searching tests not only by one angler, but by a large number of skilled men.

When that was penned I had not discovered the marrow scoop or the baby plate.

Naturally, some of my efforts to represent the nymph have been less successful than others. And though later in this volume I give particulars of the more successful dressings, I would warn my readers that patterns which are effective on Itchen and Test are not necessarily effective on other streams. Nor, indeed, is a pattern which killed yesterday necessarily effective on the same river to-day, when quite probably other species of flies are hatching or by their preponderance are exacting more of the trout's attention.

The Usk is a river on which the practice of nymph fishing has made great progress—but the range of natural

PERSONAL

upwinged flies on the Usk differs largely from that of Test or Itchen—many of the flies being larger and brighter in colour. The same is no doubt the case on other rivers. For these reasons I would urge on those who are interested to be at the pains to dress their own nymph patterns from the natural model.

IX

REACTION

In the last year or so I have, somewhat to my surprise, seen signs of a movement on the part of some chalk stream anglers to try to re-rivet upon their brethren the fetters of the exclusive dry fly, from which I had hoped that time, experience and common sense had enabled anglers to shake themselves free. But whenever I have come across anglers who wish to re-establish the exclusive dominance of the dry fly, I have almost invariably found that they ranged themselves under one or more of the following heads:

(1) Men who do not understand and will not take the trouble to learn the art of fishing the nymph.
(2) Men who find the whole fascination of chalk stream fishing in seeing the fly taken on the surface—a good enough reason for their own practice, but none for intolerance nor for restricting the practice of anglers who find an even subtler charm in taking sub-aqueously trout which, while feeding at or near the surface, are not taking the floating natural insect.
(3) Men who suppose it to be a "chuck and chance it" method of fishing the water. These are radically and ignorantly wrong, for it is nothing of the sort.
(4) Men who think it an unduly deadly method. It is too difficult an art to be that, even if the charge were true. After all, the dry fly came in as an improved and more deadly method, enabling the angler to

catch trout untakable in light or calm weather by the wet fly as then understood. Why then should an art which gives the angler a chance of taking trout for the time being untakable by the dry fly be barred?

(5) Finally (and these are the great majority), men who do not know what a nymph is like and assume that the objects commonly sold by tackle dealers as such—most of which bear no resemblance to the real insect and have whatever success they obtain simply as lures, illegitimate on chalk streams—are what is meant by nymphs. This class are justified in their objection to the use of such objects under the name of nymph or any other name, but are not justified in objecting to the use of proper representations of the natural nymph.

I cannot believe that this reaction will succeed. It is suggested that fishing the nymph is an easier matter than fishing the dry fly—but all that this boils down to is that drag makes the dry fly difficult and that the nymphs, it is said, may drag without scaring the trout. But this is all: and it is not wholly true; while the special difficulties attending fishing the nymph which are absent from dry-fly practice are ignored. It comes to this, that the dry-fly purist seeks to impose on the angler either abstention from fishing to a rising fish which is nymphing, or else the obligation of persecuting him with the futility of a floating fly while he is confining himself to subaqueous food.

Though it is claimed by those in the movement that the floating fly is the more difficult method, I can only say, speaking for myself, that if I see the trout taking the surface fly I should offer them a floater as being the easier and the obviously correct course. But I decline to be coerced into

REACTION

fishing floaters to trout which are consistently nymphing or, alternatively, into abstaining from fishing them until they have come on to surface food, which may not happen at all in the course of my day or week-end.

It is further suggested that the effect of fishing the nymph is to drive the trout to feeding deep. In my opinion this is unmitigated nonsense. On the chalk stream with which I am most familiar (having fished it from 1883 onward) the years during which I have been fishing the under-water fly and the nymph have been marked by a progressive disposition on the part of the trout to feed on nymphs just below the surface and to ignore the surface fly. It would be equally logical to say that nymph fishing would tend to drive fish to the floating fly. Before the advent of the dry fly all trout fishing with the fly, on chalk streams as well as elsewhere, was subaqueous—but the trout have never been driven to feed deep, as it is suggested they would be. *The Diary of a Test Fisherman,* covering the years 1809 to 1819, shows clearly that the writer, the Rev. Richard Durnford, knew well that his Test and Anton trout were often feeding subaqueously; and he had wonderful baskets.

Dr Mottram, once an advocate of the nymph, but in his later days a protagonist of the attack on nymph fishing, cannot put his case higher than that nymph fishing on streams where the trout can be easily caught *out* with the dry fly alone, ought not to be allowed. On such streams, who would want to fish the nymph at times when the simpler and more obvious method of the floating fly is available?

X

THE PRONOUNCEMENTS OF HALFORD

THOUGH I believe that the movement to reassert the exclusive dominance of the dry fly on chalk streams is largely due to the use by some anglers of the illegitimate lures sold as nymphs by many tackle dealers and ignorantly accepted as such by their customers, yet that is not the case put forward by the purists. The arguments adduced are based upon F. M. Halford, and I do not think therefore that the case for the nymph can be said to have been conclusively dealt with without an examination of the pronouncements thereon of Halford as its main and most authoritative opponent, both in his earlier work and also in his later works, when his doctrine had become less liberal and more and more pronouncedly purist. I am therefore inflicting on the reader a somewhat prolonged analysis of Halford's writings on this subject which I beg him not to skip, as it is vital to a correct understanding of how he came to assume his intolerant attitude on the question of fishing wet fly and nymph on chalk streams.

It is nothing but justice to say of Halford that the governing spirit of his purist doctrine was unselfishness, the desire to be fair at once to his brother angler and to the trout; and it is without any thought of imputing to him any less magnanimous motive that I feel bound to examine his pronouncements closely and to demonstrate how his failure to realise certain essential features of the situation led him, by the very fact of his magnanimity, to enunciate doctrines which experience has shown to be unsound.

I have already said that I have no quarrel whatever—on the contrary, I am in agreement with his objection to chalk stream anglers "fishing the water", searching it with a wet fly or a team of wet flies, thus catching or pricking and scaring unsizable fish, and incidentally covering as much water as would be enough for several anglers casting fly, dry or wet, or artificial nymph to individual selected feeding fish in position. But from first to last Halford never seems to have understood or believed that it was possible to direct the wet fly (or nymph) successfully to such fish when feeding subaqueously with as much precision and with as much care for the feelings and interests of the brother angler and as much consideration for unsizable fish as is displayed by the most careful purist fishing the dry fly to surface feeders. He expressed his incredulity in very definite terms at page 75 of his last work, *The Dry Fly Man's Handbook* (1913), in which he came down hard in favour of strict purism. He says:

I am told that there is a school of fly fishermen who only fish the sunk fly over a feeding fish or one in position if it will not take a floating fly. This, they urge, is a third method of wet-fly fishing, the other two being the more ordinary of *fishing the water* with sunk fly either up-stream or down-stream. Candidly, I have never seen this method in practice, and I have grave doubts as to its efficacy.

Yet years of practice of this method have made me ever more and more convinced of its soundness, particularly in cases where in place of the wet fly an appropriate pattern of nymph is presented to the feeding trout. This method, moreover, is *not* "fishing the water".

Halford died in 1913, at a date when the practice of fishing the artificial nymph was not much more than mooted, but the use of the wet fly fished up-stream or up and across to selected individual fish had been put definitely on the map; and though both in *Dry Fly Fishing in Theory and Practice* and in his final volume he had authoritatively discredited the possibility of effective representation of the natural nymph, it was the wet fly that was the enemy in the passage which I have quoted.

In the days preceding the advent of the dry fly there were no doubt exceptional fishermen who did some at least of their fishing to individual rising fish; but, taking it by and large, I infer that most of the chalk stream wet-fly fishing was done in rough windy weather with flies which searched the water, being fished dragging across and down. The Diary of the Rev. Richard Durnford, 1809 to 1819, published in 1911 by Henry Nicoll under the title, *Diary of a Test Fisherman*, speaks constantly of "a whistling wind", "a sufficient wind" and so on, and he used "a bob fly to steady the cast". In those times the angler stayed at home on still days. In his Autobiography (p. 83) Halford quotes Major Carlisle (South West) writing of the Houghton Club water in the early 'seventies.

> Trout were far easier to catch, while of those who fished, perhaps only half—maybe fewer—had any idea of dry-fly fishing, and it was a common thing to see an angler flailing away with two big flies on the thickest of gut, downstream, and to hear his complaint of not catching anything.

Coming to the Test with his dry-fly experience of the Wandle, with the restricted lengths there available for the individual angler, it is not unnatural that Halford should resent the methods of the down-stream flailer. The heavy and powerful dry-fly rods with their heavy tapered casting lines then in use by dry-fly men were utterly unsuited to present a wet fly up-stream or up and across to fish in position, and it is perhaps not unnatural that Halford should have made little or no attempt to do so. When the light rod came in in the early days of the present century, Halford fought against it and I doubt if he ever possessed a rod and line capable of first-rate up-stream wet-fly work in still weather on chalk streams. So, right through his work, whenever he speaks of the use of the wet fly on chalk streams he invariably associates it with the practice of down-stream flogging and "fishing the water" as contrasted with fishing to individual fish.

As this statement has been challenged—notably in a debate on the subject of nymph fishing in chalk streams recently held at the Fly Fishers' Club—I feel bound to produce chapter and verse in justification of it. At page 36 of *Dry Fly Fishing in Theory and Practice* (1886), in a chapter headed "Floating Flies and Sunk Flies", Halford writes:

> In principle the two methods of fishing are totally and entirely distinct. With the dry or floating fly the angler has in the first instance to find a rising fish, to note accurately the position or what is technically called "spot the rise" and to cast to this fish to the exclusion of any chance work in other parts of the stream. With the sunk or wet-fly on the other hand he casts to a likely place whether he has or has not seen a rise there (more frequently he has not) and in fact his judgment should tell him where from his knowledge of the habits of the fish they are most likely to be found in position or ready to feed. Thus wet-fly fishing is often termed "fishing the water" in contradistinction to the expression "fishing the rise" which is applied to the method of the dry-fly fisherman.

This is no doubt an excellent description of wet-fly fishing as practised on North Country and other rough rivers, but it does not seem ever to have occurred to Halford that the method of "fishing the rise" with the wet fly or nymph might be (as it has been) successfully adopted on chalk streams when the trout were seen to be feeding sub-aqueously.

THE PRONOUNCEMENTS OF HALFORD

I have already quoted at page 66 the passage from his last book, the *Handbook* (1913), in which, in spite of twenty-seven years' intervening experience, and in despite of testimony to the contrary he avowed his disbelief in such a method.

In his intervening work I have found no evidence whatever that he ever changed his mind on the subject. But his Autobiography (1903) contains a passage at pages 69 and 70 which I must quote for the sake of the comment it evokes.

I was much interested, some years since, watching a first-rate wet-fly man, a Yorkshire fisherman, on a portion of the Upper Test. His flies were olive quills of various shades, iron blues, red quills, and such patterns, all of which he used on his native streams, and were dressed with peacock quill bodies, very meagre upright wings, and a single turn of hen hackle for legs. He did not in any way practise the "chuck and chance it" plan, but moved slowly upstream, carefully studying the set of the current and quickly deciding where a feeding fish should be in each run. Sometimes it would be close under the bank, sometimes on the edge of a slack place, and sometimes on the margin of an eddy.

Whenever he had made up his mind as to the most likely spot there, he would make one, or at most two light casts, placing his fly with great accuracy and letting it drift down without drag. Now this I take it was the best possible imitation of the work of a dry-fly fisherman, except that he had not spotted the fish and his fly was not floating in the dry-fly sense. His patterns were very similar in size, colour and form, to those of the ordinary chalk stream fisherman. He used very fine drawn gut, and worked hard from morning to evening, never passing over a likely place without putting a fly into it, and very seldom losing a hooked fish.

It was in the early part of April, during strong westerly and south-westerly winds, when the hatch of duns was sparse, and when, in fact, all conditions were favourable to the sunk and unfavourable to the floating fly. He fished six days on a well-stocked reach of the river and killed in the aggregate seven trout weighing 9 lb. Candidly, I was somewhat surprised at the good result, and have often wondered whether he could repeat the performance. Of course the average weight of his fish, just over 1¼ lb., was very small for the Test, and two or three of them would have been returned by many dry-fly fishermen.

Let it be clearly understood, however, that this fisherman was most skilful and painstaking, and was a past master in the art of selecting the right spot, and in placing his fly accurately and delicately *there* at the first attempt. Had he merely fished the river up or down, or had he bungled his cast, or moved about rapidly, or, in fact, made any mistakes, I do not believe he would have killed a single trout, so that his bag represents the best possible result, under existing conditions, for a wet fly fisherman on a stream like the Upper Test.

Now on this passage I call my readers' attention to the words, "This I take it was the best possible imitation of the work of a dry-fly fisherman *except that he had not spotted the fish*". The Yorkshire fisherman in question, a Mr Reffitt —a correspondent of my own—was therefore not fishing to individual fish, but guessing, or judging if you prefer it, where the fish ought to be. He was fishing, moreover, in early April, a time of year when the rise is sparse and rarely extends over two hours, and though he fished "hard from morning to evening", we are not told that he fished to any rising fish or even saw any rise.

Halford says, "All conditions were favourable to the sunk and unfavourable to the floating fly". This brings me back to a passage in *Dry Fly Fishing* which shows pretty clearly that Halford did not know what conditions on chalk streams *were* favourable to the sunk fly. It occurs on page 39, where, after describing conditions favourable to the dry fly, Halford proceeds:

On the other hand where no rising or bulging fish are to be seen, and whence it may be inferred that the fish are not taking surface food at all, the conditions are favourable for the use of the sunk fly.

This is quite wrong. Such conditions are *not* favourable for

THE PRONOUNCEMENTS OF HALFORD

the use of the sunk fly. On chalk streams the fish must be as definitely feeding to take wet fly or nymph as to take the floater, with the difference that they are taking subaqueously; and they must be either bulging over weeds to the nymph emerging from the weeds, or taking the mature nymph on the verge of hatching. It is clear that the Rev. Richard Durnford knew this, though his most successful fishing was done in rough water.

There is another paragraph in the *Handbook* (at p. 68) in which Halford gives a description of wet-fly fishing, contrasting it with the dry fly. He says:

> The wet-fly fisherman does not as a general rule wait for a rising fish, but places his fly (he frequently uses two, three or even four) in a part of the river where, from his experience of the habits of the trout he would expect a feeding fish to be located. Some fish up-stream, some down-stream and some across the stream. In the hands of a past master it is a most scientific and under favourable conditions a very deadly method of fishing.

Now this is an excellent description of the wet-fly method as practised on North Country and other rough rivers, but it is not fair argument to contrast it with the floating fly on chalk streams. Why did he not contrast the dry fly with the modern wet fly as applied to chalk streams? I suggest that the answer is to be found in the paragraph I have already quoted from page 75 of the *Handbook*. He had "grave doubts of its efficacy". In other words, he did not believe it.

Other sentences from the same volume illustrate Halford's attitude towards the wet fly. At page 74 he writes:

> Nothing more surely tends to develop further the increasing shyness of the fish than the presence of a few persistent downstream floggers with the sunk fly.

True enough, but do we find anywhere a suspicion even

that the wet fly or nymph can be fished to subaqueously feeding fish as precisely as the dry fly to surface feeders, and that there is no need for "persistent down-stream flogging"? No.

On the next page he proceeds:

I will at once freely admit that up-stream wet-fly fishing is not so harmful on a chalk stream as the same method pursued down-stream. But in my view the continual flogging and the continual movements of the angler making his way along the bank too often in full view of the trout are however very nearly as destructive of the confidence of the fish as down-stream fishing. Then too the distance covered by the persistent flogger is so great that the limits of any ordinary length of water will be covered many times in a day's fishing.

If it be suggested that the methods there described are characteristic of the modern chalk stream angler with wet fly or nymph, I say they are unmitigated nonsense, intended by the writer to discredit a technique which he did not understand and disliked.

This brings me to the investigation of the question how it came about that a man of his high intelligence, ability and opportunities, so failed in understanding.

Let us turn back to *Dry Fly Fishing* at page 143. He is describing a cold day in May 1885.

It was a day on which a fresh breeze from the north-west was blowing, and so cold was it that, to an idler on the river-bank, it was a difficult matter to keep his hands warm; and yet the number of flies hatching was, even to one accustomed to the plentiful supply on chalk streams, something astonishing. The trout seemed to have appetites which could not be appeased, rushing about in all directions, making heavy bulges under water as they took the larvae rising from the bed of the river, or here and there just breaking the surface as they seized the fly at the very instant of its casting off the envelope in which it had passed the pupa state. This should of itself indicate the fact that it was a most unsuccessful

THE PRONOUNCEMENTS OF HALFORD

day, and that the trout could not be persuaded to look at any artificial fly, as their every movement was to secure the swiftly darting larvae when rising to the surface and before emerging from the shuck.

To dress an artificial representing the larva or pupa is difficult, but not an absolutely impossible task. Having overcome his natural repugnance to descend from what may be described as high art to the less scientific sunk-fly style of fishing, and having succeeded in turning out a fairly good imitation, the amateur is prone to imagine that he has at last solved the problem, and can, by fishing it under water, make sure of a respectable bag at a time when the fish are bulging incessantly at the natural larvae. Alas! how woefully he is *désillusionné*. *The fish will not look at this*, although it is an admirable representation, both in colour and shape, of the natural insect. And what is the reason? To elucidate this, take a handful of weed from the bed of the river and extract from it three or four specimens of the dun larvae with which it abounds; place these in a tumbler of clear water and patiently watch. Those that are nearly ready to hatch, or are rising to the surface for that purpose, seem positively electrified, every feeler or leg, and every fold or rib of their bodies, moving in an eccentric but continual motion. How is it to be expected that a timid, shy fish like a trout, who from painful daily, and even hourly, experience is warned to use the keenest of all the senses with which he has been endowed by nature, viz. his sight, for his protection, should mistake that motionless supine compound of dubbing, silk, quill, and hackle drifting helplessly and lifelessly like a log down the stream, for the active, ever-moving larva sparkling in the sunshine, and varying in colour at every motion as rays of light strike it at different angles?

Now just consider Halford's elucidation. He takes a handful of weed from the bed of the river and extracts dun larvae and finds them extremely active. I have already recounted how to the end he was in the habit of quoting G. S. Marryat's saying, "You can imitate the nymph, but you cannot imitate the wriggle", and there is a passage on page 122 of *Dry Fly Fishing* where, apropos of bulging, Halford writes:

It is my opinion that the difficulty does not lie in dressing an artificial grub fairly resembling the dun's nymph but in imparting to that imitation the motion and direction taken by the natural insect at that stage of its existence.

It does not seem to have occurred to him that though a nymph—even a nymph nearing maturity—might be highly active when taken from his shelter in the weeds it did not follow that it was always active as the moment approached for it to put off its shuck. I have shown (with reasons), in the chapter on "The Way of a Trout with a Nymph", that in these conditions it is often practically inert and that, as well observed by Dr Mottram, even when emerging from weeds on the occurrence of bulging, though it may move from side to side (possibly deflected by the changes in the current caused by the sway of the water) its motion is "quite slow and calm, not in the least fast or jerky".

I have so frequently caught bulging trout with an artificial nymph fished up-stream, and so much more frequently similarly taken trout feeding quietly under banks or in runs on the ascending nymph about to hatch, that I have no doubt whatever about the fact that there is nothing in the activity of the natural nymph to prevent the trout from taking an artificial nymph. A good imitation is in fact an excellent attraction for subaqueously feeding fish.

When however we come to examine what Halford has to say about trout feeding on nymphs in the latter conditions we find only one reference, viz. at page 125 of *Dry Fly Fishing* (1889):

> Sometimes fish, when feeding on larvae and nymphae, however, rise quietly, and do not move about much from place to place; and under these circumstances it is almost impossible to distinguish the apparent from the *bona fide* rises, except by watching intently the surface of the water with the view of making certain that the winged duns floating on the stream are being taken. One such case is brought prominently to my mind, when on a hot

THE PRONOUNCEMENTS OF HALFORD

August evening a trout rose steadily under the bank until it was almost pitch dark. For an hour or more I kept on throwing steadily, and, I am vain enough to think, without making any glaring mistake, over this fish. Commencing with a very small pale yellow dun (Flight's Fancy), then trying in succession a blue-winged olive, red quill, ginger quill, hackled-winged red spinner, Jenny spinner, and detached badger, I at length, as a last resource, put up a small silver sedge on an O hook. The very first cast secured a trout upwards of 2 lb.; and knowing that fish feeding on *curses* will occasionally, for some occult reason, take this particular pattern, I fancied that I knew all about it, and made sure that it had been feeding on these annoying little insects. On my return home an autopsy of the contents of its stomach revealed an extraordinary conglomeration of shrimps, caddis, snails, larvae, and nymphae, but not a single winged fly.[1]

Here we have Halford hammering for hours a fish which was unquestionably nymphing, offering it in succession seven different patterns of floating dun, and ultimately getting it at dusk with a sedge. It never seems to have occurred to him, either during the incident *or at any subsequent time*, to fish a trout so feeding otherwise than with the floating fly: and the only credible explanation which occurs to me is that he always believed the nymphs on which the trout were feeding were too active to be successfully represented, and that therefore the sole hope of getting such a fish was to continue trying him with a succession of patterns in the hope that ultimately he might be led to make a mistake. I also infer that the only occasions on which he tried the artificial nymph must have been on bulging fish (I will not suggest with a dragging fly), and that he failed entirely, both then and thereafter, to realise that the fish rising quietly as described were not chasing active nymphs but were feeding on floating nymphs coming up so quietly as to be

[1] This statement is repeated at pp. 167-8 of the 1902 edition without comment or enlargement.

motionless, or in other words, "practically inert". I am no purist, but I must confess it seems to me at least as unethical to hammer a nymphing trout with a succession of floating flies as to offer a nymph to a trout which is exclusively taking hatched duns, a practice which I do not advocate.

The incident quoted from page 125 of the first edition of *Dry Fly Fishing* is repeated, I believe, verbatim, in the subsequent editions—showing that Halford learned nothing from that or subsequent experience.

Before leaving this phase of the subject I have to refer to a passage on nymph fishing at pages 126-127 of the *Handbook*, where Halford writes:

With respect to the question of dressing imitations of nymphs, I have always urged that any fly-dresser who sets his mind to it can do this easily. Years and years ago Marryat and I dressed most effective patterns to represent the nymphs of duns and mayflies by tying in a few fibres of black feather at the head, constructing the fly generally with a quill body the colour of the abdomen of the natural nymph, hackle short and spare, and the whisks, which were also short, of gallina, were dyed to shade. When the body material had been tied in, the fibres of black feather were bent down into a shallow loop and fastened in at the shoulder to represent the wing cases of the natural nymph, the hackle was then turned, and the fly finished at the head.

We killed a few fish with them, but discontinued their use for two reasons. The first, that in our opinion they were essentially wet flies, and the use of them on waters reserved for dry fly only, constituted a breach of the ethics of the dry fly. The second, which may possibly be a more cogent reason in the minds of many modern anglers, was that wherever and whenever we used them we found that the number of fish hooked and lost was out of all proportion to the total bag, and that the fish rapidly became inordinately shy and unapproachable. This, I think, sums up the position fairly from the dry-fly purist's point of view, and I can only advise my readers to abstain from trying bulging fish either on their own or their friends' fisheries in all cases where the use of the floating fly is considered *de rigueur*.

THE PRONOUNCEMENTS OF HALFORD

I find this statement hard to reconcile with the passage which I quoted at page 73 from page 144 of *Dry Fly Fishing*, where Halford says, "The fish will not look at this, although it is an admirable representation, both in colour and shape, of the natural insect". I have grounds for knowing that the date when Marryat was dressing artificial nymphs was before 1883, as he gave patterns to my friend, the late Rev. E. R. J. Nicolls, while he was fishing, during the tenancy of Marryat and Francis Francis, the same length of the Itchen which Mr Irwin E. B. Cox took over at the beginning of 1883—and which I have been fishing ever since. I can only account for the statement by assuming a lapse of memory on Halford's part, since upwards of twenty-seven years had elapsed since the publication of *Dry Fly Fishing* and sixteen years since the death of Marryat. Assuming that he caught a few, the statement of the disproportionate number of fish hooked and lost would suggest that the experiments were made fishing down-stream to bulgers with drag and not up-stream or up and across to trout quietly taking the hatching mature nymph.

Here again I must point out that Halford's advice is to abstain from trying *bulging fish*, once more ignoring the case of the trout taking the mature nymph quietly under banks and elsewhere which are the best trout to assail with the artificial nymph.

In further endeavour to understand Halford's mind on the subject let me quote some further passages—the first from page 239 of *Dry Fly Fishing* in the chapter on Autopsy:

> It has been clearly shown that by far the larger proportion of the contents of the stomach of a trout or grayling consists of larvae, nymphae, caddis, shrimps, etc., *which are normally in the middle or lower depths of the water.*

The italics are mine, and as regards nymphs, though

most of their lives are spent in weeds and mud on the lower depths of the water, from the angler's point of view the times when they are being taken by trout, so as to give the angler a chance of interposing his imitation, are (1) when the trout are bulging to them over weeds, and (2) when the trout are taking them just under the surface on their way to hatch out. The numerous examinations which I have made of the contents of the stomachs of trout tell me that only a small proportion of the nymphs there found are taken in the middle and lower depths of the water.

At this point it may be convenient if I refer to another statement of Halford's from page 240 of the same chapter. He writes:

In any case it must be remembered that the presence in an autopsy of nymphae just on the point of changing to the winged fly indicates that the fish, *although as a rule under such conditions looking downwards*, has yet followed the *active* nymph towards the surface.

This is another misapprehension on Halford's part. Apart from the fact that the nymph under such conditions is *not* active but in general practically inert, the trout, as clearly demonstrated by Colonel E. W. Harding in *The Fly Fisher and the Trout's Point of View*, is *not* looking downward, but lies with his gaze fixed upward and forward on the mirror-like underside of the surface up-stream of his window, and sees the approaching nymphs reflected in the surface, and rises gently to meet them, preferably near the point where reflection and reality are about to merge.

The paragraph at page 239 goes on:

At the first glance a natural deduction from this would be that the sunk fly would be more likely to tempt than the floating ones. Very possibly many of the sparsely dressed patterns used more generally in the North for wet-fly fishing are taken for some forms of larvae . . . and it has been confidently said by North Country

THE PRONOUNCEMENTS OF HALFORD

anglers of great experience that an adept of this style could work sad havoc on some of the well-stocked shallows of the chalk streams. Unfortunately very few of the disciples of the dry fly practice, even if they understand, the art of fishing the sunk fly, which may account for the fact that as a general rule when tried in the Hampshire streams it has not proved successful. It would be well for a first-rate performer to pay a visit to the Test or Itchen and thoroughly thrash out the point.

In this connection I may mention that I have had a good North Country angler on my own length of the Itchen (which the late William Senior described as the most difficult water he knew) and, fishing with nymphs lightly dressed according to my methods, and presenting them up-stream or across to trout feeding on nymphs, he has made baskets which would have done any Hampshire angler credit.

Halford proceeds:

I confess to feeling grave doubts as to the result. If it is to be judged by any attempt heard of up to the present time, it is foredoomed; if on the other hand previous failures have been due to want of knowledge and experience on the part of the fisherman, it is quite on the cards that it might revolutionise the whole art of fly fishing as practised in Hampshire.

If, however, as I am inclined to predict, there should be a fiasco the natural question is to enquire whether it is possible to take these wary fish when feeding under water with an imitation of their natural food. The larva has been frequently imitated and has occasionally done well, but strange to relate on the days when it has done well, it has almost invariably turned out that other fishermen have done well with the dry fly.

That is a general statement which it is impossible to check. It is not my experience. I have known many occasions when the nymph alone was being taken, the hatched dun being wholly neglected, and but few occasions when trout feeding on the surface fly were wholly unattracted by the nymph.

Halford proceeds, "It has generally been in early spring when the trout are comparatively easy to catch". I do not agree. I have used the nymph successfully right through the season, even in the most difficult days of July and August, and have taken some of my largest trout on it.

Again Halford, misled no doubt by the contrast of dry-fly methods with the superseded wet-fly methods in use on chalk streams, was led to infer that still days and hot sun and clear water are fatal to the wet-fly (or nymph) fisher. He writes on page 29 of *Dry Fly Fishing*:

> As to conditions of weather, on the stillest days with the hottest sun and in the clearest water, the fish are generally on the surface where the wet-fly fisher would consider the conditions most unpropitious and unlikely on such days to kill fish is most gratifying to the angler's bump of self-esteem; and often the largest and most suspicious fish feeding under such conditions seem quite guileless and fall victims to the art of the dry-fly fisherman.

I would assure Halford, if he were here to receive my assurance, that on such days when the trout are taking the mature nymph rising to hatch, the like success may be predicated for the nymph fisher or the wet-fly fisher casting the right pattern of nymph or wet fly to selected individual feeding fish. In such conditions it is often the case that the trout are exclusively nymphing and are letting the floating natural dun go by; but they will take an appropriately dressed nymph where they would ignore the artificial floating dun.

In other places Halford suggests that only small (often unsizable) fish are taken with the sunk fly and that many are pricked and lost. On page 71 of the *Handbook* he pictures as typical an angler who

> will proceed to the upper limit of the fishery and flog it steadily down with wet fly. He will probably see some fish following his

THE PRONOUNCEMENTS OF HALFORD

fly, occasionally even plucking at it and getting pricked; a few, but a very small proportion being landed, and of these the vast majority yearlings or two-year-olds. Perchance he may succeed in getting two or three killable trout, but these as a rule are only just up to or possibly under the legal limit of the fishery.

I need hardly say that this is not a method which is within my contemplation as legitimate wet-fly or nymph fishing. Fishing and searching the water with a dragging wet fly is undoubtedly apt to lead to the catching or pricking or scaring of unsizable fish. But the illegitimacy of such practices affords no reason for forbidding the use of the nymph or wet-fly cast up-stream or across to subaqueously feeding fish. And nowhere do I find in Halford's books any reference to such methods except the passage from the *Handbook*, quoted at page 66, in which Halford not only expresses his lack of belief in them but says he *had never seen the method in practice*. Nevertheless it is a great method and a fascinating one, and it has brought me the great bulk of my largest trout and has greatly increased my score of 2-pounders on a river where 2-pounders are by no means everyday fish.

On page 45 of *Dry Fly Fishing* Halford says:

On one point all must agree, viz. that fishing up-stream with the finest of gut and floating the tiniest of flies is far more exacting and requires in many respects more skill than the *fishing of the water* as practised by the wet-fly fisherman.

Exactly the same claim may be made for nymph fishing as defined and advocated by me.

The modern wet-fly fisher and the nymph fisher on chalk streams who know their business are *not* "fishing the water" but casting to individual selected subaqueously feeding fish in position.

On the question of comparative skill as between that

method and the dry fly I do not wish to dogmatise. I do not pretend to be an exceptionally skilful fisherman. My practice, like that perhaps of many other anglers, often falls short of my theoretical knowledge. But I may say I have heard not a few skilled dry-fly fishermen confess that to fish the artificial nymph according to my method was beyond them.

I do not think it necessary to pitch my case for fishing the artificial nymph to nymphing trout so high as to say that it revolutionises the entire practice of Hampshire trout fishing. In fact it leaves the correct practice of dry-fly fishing intact for all occasions where it is applicable, but it *does* fill a gap in the armament of the chalk stream angler, in providing him with a clean and sportsmanlike method of meeting those hours (and it is often those days) when trout are nymphing and letting the upwinged dun go by disregarded.

My claim therefore for nymph fishing is that it enables the angler to approach a nymph-taking trout with success in bright weather and smooth water in conditions which authority had hitherto held to be almost impossible, that it enables an angler to deal with a nymph-feeding trout, which would either be hammered in vain by the dry-fly fisherman, or else, if he were a real understanding purist, be left despairingly alone; and that thus the method of nymph fishing which my good friend the late H. T. Sheringham called "exact wet-fly fishing" constitutes as real if not as great an advance in the art of fly fishing as the dry fly indubitably did. It has the merit of superseding or getting over serious difficulties and limitations of the dry fly and so adding to the angler's chances of sport.

Though I have subjected the works of Halford to so critical an analysis, it is only because he has been beyond question the dominant writer on chalk stream fishing, and it is only just to say that no other writers on that subject ever seem to have suspected the propensity of chalk stream trout to feed largely on nymphs (outside the practice of bulging) prior to my calling attention to the subject—or even (apart from Dr J. C. Mottram, Eric Taverner and Colonel E. W. Harding) since.

H. S. Hall, who was Halford's contemporary and wrote of the dry fly in the Badminton Library just before *Floating Flies and How to Dress Them* appeared and took the angling world by storm, is silent on the subject. Viscount Grey seems to have had no suspicion of the state of the case, nor had Major Fisher (*Rod and River*, 1892), nor Lord Buxton. Earl Hodgson, though he mocked at the pretensions of the dry-fly purist, gives no reason for the faith that was in him. Passing outside the chalk stream area we find nothing on the subject in Stewart's *Practical Angler*, nothing in David Foster's *Scientific Angler*, nothing in E. M. Tod and nothing in any of the wet-fly authorities. The subject is in fact relatively a new one, and that must be my justification for inflicting yet another book on the patient fly-fishing public.

XI

PROS AND CONS

THE dry-fly man, after the long innings he has had, is often not of an open mind, and is unwilling to give up the exclusive doctrine of the dry fly, and he therefore seeks for arguments to justify it.

If he insists that trout will not look at the nymph and I prove the contrary, then he claims:

(1) That nymph fishing is easier than the dry fly, mainly because of the matter of drag;
(2) That it kills more fish, *i.e.* is too deadly and leaves too few fish for the relatively finer art of the dry fly;
(3) That persistence in the use of the nymph drives the fish to feed deep by killing off those which feed just under the surface;
(4) That trout feed mainly on nymphs and only take floating flies as a sort of sport or delicacy and that it is right that there should be one part of their habitat where they can feed with confidence and need have no fear of the angler's wiles;
(5) That for all or some of these reasons the use of the nymph on chalk streams is ethically wrong.

To all this the nymph fisher replies:

(1) If it is so much easier than the dry fly, why do so **few** relatively practise it—and still fewer competently? As a matter of fact it has difficulties of its own, not excluding the matter of drag. Moreover many anglers

refuse to try it as being beyond them. Indeed there must be hundreds of chalk stream anglers who are unable to distinguish between the rise of a trout to the floating natural insect and his rise to a nymph, and so go on despairingly and vainly hammering nymphing trout with floating flies.

(2) If it kills more fish, is that an objection? Why, pray, was the dry fly advocated but because it provided a method of killing fish not amenable to the previous practice of the wet fly? Well, nymph fishing provides a method of taking trout when they are not amenable to the attractions of the dry fly.

(3) I am afraid the answer to the dry-fly man's third point is the rude one—"Skittles". As well say that the persistent presentation of the dry fly has driven trout to nymphing. My own observation is that on the waters where I have been using the nymph for years the growing tendency of the trout has been to nymph more and more and to do so at and just under the surface.

(4) If one analyses the contents of the stomach of a trout, and finds, as he constantly will find, that it consists almost entirely of nymphs, it will be obvious that in confining himself to the floating fly the angler will either be condemning himself to inactivity for the greater part if not all of his fishing day or be casting floating flies to trout which are feeding exclusively below the surface. If and when trout will not feed on the surface, the only way to get them is to fish them where they are feeding. Of course any riparian owner or lessee may make any rules he likes for his water, and his guests and any guest accepting his hospitality must in honour and decency abide by his

conditions. But in the absence of such conditions, it is trying poor angling nature and patience rather high to insist that one is bound to refrain from offering his ephemeral simulacrum wet or from fishing at all on occasions when the trout are feeding subaqueously. For, make no mistake, trout will go on for hours nymphing, and will either take no notice of the dry fly or will be put down by it if it drags, and in such conditions it is unethical on the dry-fly man's own principles for him to go on hammering with a dry fly a fish which is consistently confining himself to nymphs. The reasonable practice is to offer the fish the best possible representation of what he is taking where he is taking it, whether above water or below.

One angler of my acquaintance goes so far as to argue that to fish the nymph is not fly fishing, a nymph being no more a fly than a caterpillar is a moth or a butterfly. Well, the term "fly fishing" was applied to wet-fly work on chalk streams long years, even centuries, before the advent of the dry fly, at times when the wet fly was certainly often taken for a nymph, though no doubt very few of those who used it realised the fact. The modern practice is merely to use a better ephemeral representation with better knowledge, enabling the angler to do in still water what previously required a ruffle; and no nymph fisher need have any ill-conscience about following in the footsteps of the great anglers of the past.

Halford's argument against the use of the artificial nymph was, "It was a breach of the ethics of the dry fly".

(If that means that he was fishing waters where it was a condition that the dry fly only might be used, it is irrelevant as an argument against the use of the nymph on waters where that condition is not explicitly or implicitly imposed.)

He advises his readers to abstain from "trying *bulging* fish either on their own or their friends' waters *where the floating fly is considered de rigueur*—a question-begging phrase. No decent angler would break conditions laid down by or implicit in his leave. But the opinion is quite irrelevant to the question whether nymph fishing to fish feeding on nymphs is itself a fair and reasonable practice. The decision does not depend on reason, but on the will of the owner of the fishing.

It is noteworthy that this advice of Halford applies to fishing for "bulging" trout. His description of bulging trout is to be found a little further on in the *Dry Fly Man's Handbook*, page 116, where he says:

When feeding on larvae or nymphae it (the trout) is described as "bulging", from its motion through the water.

At page 125 there follows a more elaborate description:

He will see movements at or near the surface of a pronounced nature caused by fish ploughing their way through the water upwards, moving from side to side and occasionally he may even distinguish the head of a fish just showing above the water. . . . The fish are busily engaged in chasing and securing the active nymphs, coming up through the water to the surface.

Not a word, it will be observed, about the far more common case when trout are lying in runs under the banks, or between weeds in the open, and meeting quietly and without pursuit or excitement the nymphs brought to them by the current, and letting the hatched duns go by them unnoticed.

I suggest that the natural course is to offer the fish the best possible representation of what he is feeding on where he is taking it, whether on or below the surface.

PROS AND CONS

In the Debate which took place on February 1938 in the Fly Fishers' Club on the subject of "Nymph Fishing in Chalk Streams" the protagonist of the purists argued with a great show of authority that I was wrong and Halford right on every point on which I had challenged his dicta, in connection with nymph fishing—particularly on the question of the activity of the mature nymph on its way up to hatch—(I have already dealt with this aspect of the case). And then he went on to quote cases in which he claimed that first-rate Test fisheries had been ruined by the use of the nymph. It did not seem to strike him (or his hearers except me) that if Halford was right and the trout would not look at the artificial nymph, it would be curious that the fish should have been so affected by the use of the nymph that they (though of course not caught with the nymph) should have become unamenable to the temptation of the dry fly. Had they been scared out of the lengths in question or had they become so nervous that they had been driven to bottom feeding? Information on these points was not afforded.

Of course Halford was wrong in saying that the trout would not look at the artificial nymph. Not only I, but many others, have proved that over and over again. Therefore the grounds for objecting to the use of the nymph had to be shifted.

XII

HOOKS

THE bodies of most nymphs being relatively long and straight, I recommend for the dressing of their representations patterns of hooks with a longish straight shank and a sufficient but not too wide a gape. For nymphs of sizes No. 0 new notation, or No. 15 old notation, and upwards, the older Pryce-Tannatt down-eyed round bend was ideal. It is, I believe, no longer obtainable, but an almost identical round bend is readily procurable. In the sizes Nos. 15, 16 and 17, Pennell's down-eyed sneck bends are excellent. Down-turned-eyed hooks show far less of a disposition to make the fly skirt than do hooks with upturned eyes. These patterns take and maintain an exceptionally good grip.

I do not care about the Limerick bend for nymph patterns, the bare part of the hook being much more obvious than I like.

Before Bartleets became amalgamated with or absorbed in Milwards, they used to make a series of small down-eyed sneck-bend hooks of very fine wire but great strength, and a feature of them was that the more the trout pulled the deeper the hook buried. The series of them ran about a size smaller than the corresponding numbers in the old notation and the most useful sizes were Nos. 14, 15, 16 and 17, the first being equivalent to a small No. 0 or 15 Carlisle, and the smallest to a 0000. On the last-named size I have killed trout of 3 lb. 2 oz. and 2 lb. 15 oz. (among others) and have had to cut the hook out of the fish when landed. But

I fear that these wonderful hooks are no longer obtainable. They were never so good during or after the war as before it. On the whole therefore for the smaller sizes of nymph I do not think the angler can do much better than use the down-eyed Pennell sneck, and No. 15 is about the largest size suitable for chalk streams, but for the Usk or other rivers where the natural flies, and therefore the nymphs, run larger, a down-eyed round bend of sizes No. 1, 2 or even 3 may not be too big.

XIII

HACKLES FOR NYMPHS

It is obvious that if one's artificial nymph is to bear any precise relation to the natural insect it is to represent, the hackles must be very short. Yet I have seen illustrations of so-called nymphs in angling books pretending to authority with hackles even longer in proportion to the body than might be found in a fully hackled North Country pattern. Whatever merits these patterns may possess, they do not represent nymphs.

To enable the nymph to go under at once on hitting the surface, the hackle must be soft, either a hen's or at worst a soft or henny cockerel's—though it should be kept from clinging to the body by the pad of dubbing close up behind it.

It would be useless to expect to find suitable hackles among those supplied by dealers by the packet of a dozen or a hundred. There is a chance that some few may be found if one buys by the neck—especially where the hackles are left on the skin. But the amateur will be best suited if he picks his nymph hackles from the necks of suitable birds at his poulterer's. He should bear in mind that it is much easier to pick them too long than too short.

A friend who is a first-rate angler both on the rough rivers of the North and on chalk streams, and is a confirmed user of the nymph on the latter, expresses the view that on rough shallow streams a long-hackled fly is more paying than a short-hackled nymph. This may be because a kicking mobile hackle on a rough stream is more apt to attract the attention of the trout than a strict representation of the nymph. But he would, I am sure, agree that the mobile-hackled pattern does not in fact represent a nymph but a winged fly caught and tumbled by the current, probably in the very act of hatching. Another first-rate angler of my acquaintance finds nymphs dressed after my prescription more effective than hackled flies on the same class of rough stream, and in lakes.

In patterns of some nymphs which are dark at the thorax and light in the legs a rather larger hackle may be used if a dark-centred feather be selected to cover and blend with the pad of dubbing which represents the thorax, the lighter points of the hackle representing the legs.

The legs of nymphs are often dark. Those that are pale are usually dull in colour—but in collecting hackles no shade should be neglected. The legs and whisks of the Blue-winged Olive have a definite freckle in them, but it is hard to find either cock or hen hackles with the appropriate freckle in them sufficiently close. Partridge hackles have the freckle too widely spaced and are too brown. It occurs to me that the tips of the mallard breast feather dyed as used for Mayfly wings and tied in in a small bunch and divided might serve.

Poultry hackles are not the only suitable feathers. Short scapular feathers of the thrush, the hen blackbird, the missel thrush, the landrail and other small wild fowl make quite useful substitutes and have the added advantage of being thicker in the individual fibre than poultry hackles and therefore more like the legs of the natural nymph.

I have often seen it stated that the spider patterns of the North of England and Southern Scotland are "exactly like nymphs". They are not so, except possibly when fished down-

HACKLES FOR NYMPHS

stream with a drag which makes the hackle hug the body. They are far more probably suggestive of the subimago caught and tumbled by the stream in the very act of hatching. The old-fashioned winged patterns with the wings, thin slips of feather, lying close over the back, with the hackle sloping back close to the hook, so as to ensure a "good entry" when fished down-stream, or with a drag, were much more like nymphs.

XIV

DRESSING METHODS

THOUGH, as Halford says in more than one of his books, the dressing of a nymph (to resemble the natural insect) is not a difficult matter, it must not be assumed that what when dry looks to the eye a good representation is necessarily so in fact. When wetted it may look very different.

I therefore venture to put before my readers a few matters which my experience of a good many years suggests should not be neglected.

In the first place most of the nymphs, excluding those of the Blue-winged Olive and flat or crawling nymphs like those of the March Brown and *Rhithrogena semicolorata* (yellow upright), are long, thin and taper. In tying them therefore it is well to do so on hooks with, relatively, a good length of shank and a bend differing from the Limerick, which shows too much metal behind the tying. See Chapter XII on Hooks, page 91.

With the actual natural nymph to be represented floating under one's eye in a baby plate or a white saucer, the length of hook shank necessary to give room for the thorax and abdomen can be exactly ascertained, by laying the hook alongside the actual natural nymph. In the representation it is well to get the actual outline and taper as correct as possible. And it may be borne in mind that the natural nymph, floating in the basin, having probably been absorbed by the trout when it was just on the verge of hatching, is the full size to which it can attain. For the comfort of the angler it may be mentioned that a nymph, since it has a shuck to shed, is necessarily larger than the insect which, but for an unkind fate, would have emerged from that shuck.

Observing the natural nymphs floating in the baby plate or saucer, the first point which strikes one is that the general effect of them is darker than one would have expected; and the next is that in nymphs the thorax is essentially opaque, while the abdomen is in almost all cases more or less translucent. There is no difficulty about getting the thorax of your artificial nymph opaque.

I regard it however as of much consequence to suggest that translucency in the representation of the abdomina in the artificial nymphs. This effect may be obtained by various means. One of these involves the use of quills for bodies—but the fish will only see the translucent effect of the quill in certain lights. Passing the fish on one side it may look to the fish at once translucent and natural. On any other approach it may look dead and opaque. The effect of translucency of the quill may be heightened by the winding of fine gold or silver wire at intervals corresponding with the segmentation of the abdomen of the natural insect. Some of the nymphs with brown abdomina are well suggested by the quills from the side of the stalk of the eye feather of the peacock, stripped of its flues, of course. In tying these patterns the tying silk used should be purple or brownish grey, well waxed. This is the quill used in the Devonshire Blue Upright when correctly tied.

Most artificial nymphs however are dressed with a fur or wool dubbing—fur or wool being so extraordinarily translucent as to let the colour of the underlying tying silk be seen through it, and having the further advantage of taking up water readily. Seal's fur, with or without an admixture of some soft fur like hare's poll, to enable it to be spun easily, is exceptionally full of light. A gold rib is however almost essential to keep this somewhat stubborn material in place. This observation does not of course apply to the soft silky cream-coloured down of the baby seal. I believe that that is found beneath the coarser fibres of seal's fur usually used for fly dressing. Of course dubbing can only be laid on over a basis of tying silk.

For this reason it is well to study the underlying colour of the spinners of the natural insects of the same species, and to suggest that colour as the base colour of one's nymph by the use of appropriate tying silk. But as I said at the opening of this chapter it does not follow that because when, out of the water, an artificial nymph is dry it looks a good imitation, it will do so when it is wet. I have used opossum fur to suggest the body of a pale nymph and found that though when dry it seemed very life-like, when wet it was quite unlike the natural insect. That is only an example of what I mean. So the dresser should soak his imitation thoroughly and, laying it alongside of the natural insect in the water in the plate, not rest satisfied until the colour of the imitation is so exact that, if his artificial were placed among the nymphal contents of the trout's stomach, it would, at first sight at any rate, only be distinguishable from the natural insect by the presence of the hook. And here let me say that this precision of dressing *is* worth while. Some natural nymphs have the appearance of bleeding at the head and thorax. An exceptionally killing pattern (No. XV, p. 128 represents this species. It may also be nicely suggested by a body of top material with little red seal's fur in the mixture.

The usual range of furs may be employed, but in addition to mole, hare's ear and poll, rabbit's poll and belly and opossum, fox and English blue squirrel, I like to have a supply of the soft creamy fur from the skin of a baby seal. It matches some of the paler nymph bodies excellently. Other parts of the hare are also very useful for abdomina, while the darker furs suggest wing cases.

The abdominal parts of the body of the nymph may however in some patterns be suggested by floss or artificial silk. On no account should there be any tying silk, waxed or unwaxed, underneath the floss or artificial silk in such patterns. That puts an end at once to translucency. A degree of it can however be retained if the floss or other silk be tied in at the shoulder after the whisks (with the short waste end pointing towards the bend of the hook) then wound over the bare hook to the bend, passed under the whisks, then over and back to the shoulder, where it is secured. I have not found a gold or silver wire ribbing of any value in nymphs dressed with floss or artificial silk bodies. If the hook shank be first painted with the opaque white enamel called Cellire, the floss or artificial silk wound over it will necessarily look lighter than when wound on a bare hook. But on a bare hook there is still a good deal of translucency; just as when dyed gut or horsehair is wound on a bare hook the metal is not seen through it.

Bodies of dyed gut and horsehair are, to my mind, too hard to be satisfactory, though they look well.

Other bodies with some degree of translucency may be made with various herls. Of these the best I know is from the heron in various shades of blue, which, when dyed in a solution of picric acid or in a decoction of onion skin in vinegar, produce a beautiful series of semi-translucent olives. The next best herl I know is a brownish blue feather from the domestic goose similarly treated. Both these herls are tender and require to be protected by having wound

DRESSING METHODS

over them some turns of fine gold wire or yellow silk, the wire being the more effective. The segmentation of the body of the insect is thus suggested.

When natural nymphs are closely inspected there will be found along the body certain breathing apparatus known as branchiae. If it be desired to reproduce the effect of these, it is possible to do so by using for the body material certain quills which, on being wound, show at the edge of each turn an effect very similar to the branchiae on the natural insect. An example of the kind of feather is the red wing-feather of the peacock, dyed olive in picric acid or otherwise. Another example is the queer grey feather which the peacock erects behind his brilliant eyed tail feathers to keep them standing. This grey feather, when dyed olive and wound on, a single strand at a time, produces quite a good branchial effect. But it is a very tender feather and needs to be fortified with gold or silver wire. Another method is to wind a hackle all down the body and to cut the fibres closely.

India-rubber bodies, especially if tied with thin rubber such as is used in toy balloons, have an extremely life-like appearance—but I never did any good with them and the india-rubber tends to deliquesce and perishes rapidly, so that these patterns cannot be dressed for stock.

Nymphs ribbed with gold or silver wire do not keep very well, the wire tarnishing and losing brilliance and seldom lasting bright into a second season. It is better therefore to dress such nymphs fresh and fresh as they are needed.

In tying nymph patterns it is well not to let the tying silk show except at the head and the tail—and then only if in harmony with the general effect—as otherwise it gives an unfinished effect.

This is particularly conspicuous in quill bodies. For a

quill body made with a brown strand from the side of the stalk of the eyed feather of the peacock's tail, I have recommended that the tying silk to be used should be either what is known to fly dressers as purple or a well-waxed brownish grey, or some such neutral shade. For the pale shades of blue quill bodies grey silk with or without a shade of brown is harmonious.

Finally, whisks should be kept short, only long enough to help the hook to swim naturally in the water; and the hackles to represent the legs of the insect should be short and sparsely tied, not more than two turns at most (better one turn in most cases), and they should be close up against and supported by the dubbing which suggests the wing cases.

I am in favour of finishing (whether with the whip finish or two half hitches) with the hackle close to the eye of the hook, with just enough room for the knot of the gut to be nestling on the hackle.

The wing cases of the natural nymph are quite a definite feature of his make-up. So when first I began to attempt serious representations of the natural insect I thought it essential to tie in slips of feather of a different colour from—darker than—the body material, and I even tried using the uncut tips of the same feather to represent the insect's legs. Two methods of nymph building of this type are described and illustrated at pages 124 and 128 of *The Way of a Trout with a Fly*. A realisation however that the legs of the nymph almost invariably differ in colour from the wing cases led me to use a third method—tying in a hackle as the first step and winding it at the shoulder as the last step in the process prior to bringing the wing case material over the back, whipping it down behind the eye, cutting away the waste and finishing with the whip finish and a touch of varnish.

DRESSING METHODS

Another method, enabling one to use feathers of birds other than poultry at once for legs and wing cases was as follows:

Having selected your hackle, draw back all the fibres except the extreme tip, cut away the tip close and shake back the fibres to their natural position. Then, having first formed and completed the body of your nymph, wind the silk within three turns of the eye, lay the hackle with the underside upward on the hook, tie it down with two or three turns of the silk, pull the hackle by the stalk so as to leave only enough length for the legs projecting. Then whip over the hackle to the end of the body—secure the work with a half hitch, spin on the dubbing for the thorax and wind to near the eye. Then bring the hackle by the stalk over the thorax so as to divide the points of the hackle fibres right and left as nearly equally as possible, then tie down the hackle and stalk at the eyes and finish with the whip finish. This is a good method for such a pattern as the Iron Blue tied with a hackle of cock Jackdaw's throat (Pattern X, p. 114).

I found however that all these methods, except, perhaps, the last, produced an effect heavier and clumsier than was consistent with quite a good representation of the natural nymph, and I took to suggesting the wing cases by spinning on a patch of dubbing darker than the body material behind the hackle, which had the effect of keeping the hackle, wound at the head, from clinging to the body, and of representing the wing cases quite effectively in moving water. This method of tying has served me well, producing a far more delicate nymph-like effect than any of the other processes and proving highly acceptable to the trout—and big trout at that.

Since 1910 I have had over a quarter of a century's

concentrated experience of fishing the artificial nymph when the trout appeared to me to be feeding subaqueously, and I think I may claim to have made definite progress in the evolution of successful dressings of representations of the natural nymph, especially since I took to the use of the marrow scoop for extracting the contents of the stomachs of trout and of the white enamelled cup by the water side and of the baby plate at home for washing out and identifying the items of these contents.

It may be convenient if I here describe my latter-day process in detail:

(1) Fix a down-eyed hook of appropriate size and length in the vice.
(2) Select tying silk of appropriate colour for the body, double it round the bend of the hook—spin it in a twist and wax it with colourless wax.
(3) Unspin the waxed silk. Take the short end between left forefinger and thumb and lay it over the hook against the eye.
(4) Whip three turns from right to left over the short end and twitch or cut off the short waste end.
(5) Whip on the selected hackle for the legs with the stalk towards the tail and wind silk to middle of body.
(6) Snap or cut off the stalk of the hackle and wind silk to within three or four turns of the bend.
(7) Pick two or three fibres of the whisk feather (Gallena is as good as anything, having a valuable degree of stiffness which is not excessive) and pass the roots *under* the hook. The first turn of the silk should bring them neatly on top of the hook. The natural insect has short whisks and the artificial should have short whisks too, but not quite so short as some of the

DRESSING METHODS

natural nymphs have — the slightly longer whisks helping to keep the hook on a level keel instead of sinking tail first. Two more turns of silk and a touch of celluloid varnish secure the whisks, and the waste ends can be cut or broken off or left to be tied in with the dubbing or floss or quill so as to assist the taper of the body.

(8) If gold or silver wire or silk is to be used as ribbing, it should be bound in at this stage, lying along the body and pointing over the whisks.

(9) Next, if the body is to be quill or herl or floss silk, it is bound in similarly.

(10) The tying silk is then wound to the shoulder, and

(11) The quill or herl or floss is wound on and secured at the shoulder and followed by the ribbing, and the excess is cut away.

(12) If the body is to be dubbing, then, instead of steps (10) and (11) the dubbing is spun on the tying silk, tapering from tail to shoulder and wound.

(13) The ribbing (if any) is then wound on and secured.

(14) A short length of darker dubbing to match and suggest the wing cases of the natural nymph is then spun on the tying silk, wound to the root of the hackle, and secured with one half hitch.

(15) The hackle is then wound in front of the thorax, not more than two turns, the tying silk is passed twice through it and is secured by two half hitches or a whip finish at the eye. A touch of celluloid varnish makes all secure and the waste end of the silk is cut away and the nymph is complete.

Some of the nymphs require different coloured tying silks for body and thorax. In such cases one cuts away the body tying silk after securing the body material, waxes a short length of the appropriate silk for the thorax, winds it over the root of the hackle to the lower end of the thorax, and then steps Nos. 13 to 15 follow.

If care be taken not to overdress the nymph and to secure the right taper of the body and the correct bulk of the pad of dubbing which is to suggest the wing cases, it is wonderful what a lifelike representation of the nymph may be secured.

I re-emphasise that in tying nymphs the tier should choose his tying silk with due regard to the under or essential colour of the body of the nymph he is representing and that on occasion he should use different colours for thorax and abdomen. The under or essential colour is likely to be that of the spinner, *i.e.* the mature insect. As I have said before, the abdomen of the natural nymph is in many cases more or less translucent—the thorax is generally substantially opaque. In a number of nymphs, as in their subimagines, the eyes are of a definitely bright colour, such as red; and it can do no harm, and may conceivably do good, to reproduce this feature in the artificial nymph.

Some tiers dress nymphs with nothing but the tying silk to represent the abdomen, with or without rib, and in this instance no special precaution is needed unless a different tying silk be used for the thorax. Floss bodies—if the floss be laid over the tying silk—should have tying silk matching the floss body as precisely as possible and waxed with clear colourless wax. But a better plan is to tie in the whisks at the shoulder with the silk to be used for the thorax, then to tie in the floss with a short waste end towards the bend. Next to wind the floss over the whisks and the waste end of floss to the tail, then once under the whisks and back over the shank to the shoulder, when the floss is secured and

DRESSING METHODS

the end cut away. The dubbing for the thorax is then spun on the hackle, wound and secured, and the nymph is finished in the usual way.

It will be seen that these nymph patterns are very simple and can be rapidly tied—half a dozen, or more, may be constructed in an hour—and if they are built, as they should be, with the natural insect as model floating under one's eye in a baby plate to be matched in length, colour and proportions, one may justly hope for sport with them on those many occasions when the trout are taking nymph just under the surface in preference to the floating fly. In a recent week-end in the three brace from $1\frac{1}{2}$ lb. to 3 lb. 5 oz. which I killed with artificial nymph I found three winged flies only (one a spinner) among masses of nymph! and this is by no means a unique experience.

XV

PATTERNS

THE following are, to the date of writing, the most successful dressings of nymphs (built to suggest the natural insect), which I have so far evolved from my chalk stream experience. They are not put forward as standard patterns either for the chalk streams or other rivers. I have no doubt that in time they will be improved upon. Certainly on some other rivers, of which the Usk may be taken as an example, the upwinged duns and their nymphs differ considerably, and in the Usk are a good deal larger and brighter than the Hampshire insects. Moreover, in the chalk streams (and no doubt elsewhere) nymphs of the same species differ in colour according to conditions which are not yet understood, and may be of soil, light, food, habitat or what not. The reader must therefore attribute to this fact the differing dressings attributed to the nymph of the same natural fly. The materials are specified in the order in which they should be used.

LARGE DARK OLIVE OF SPRING

I. *April and Early May*

Hook.—No. 1 or 2 down-eyed round bend, or No. 14 down-eyed Pennell sneck.

Tying Silk.—Full yellow, waxed with brown harness-maker's wax.

Hackle.—Dark blue dun hen, or cockerel with woolly centre, the centre covering the dubbing suggests the wing cases and the points suggesting the legs.

Whisk.—Two or three strands of dark *un*speckled neck feathers of the cock Gallena (guinea-fowl) dyed dark greenish.
Rib.—Fine gold wire.
Body.—Darkest green olive seal's fur tapered from tail to shoulder and there definitely thickened.

Medium Olive Dun

Following the Large Dark Olive of spring and continuing through the season.

II. *Early in Season*

Hook.—No. 1 down-eyed round bend or No. 15 down-eyed Pennell sneck.
Tying Silk.—Primrose, waxed with clear colourless wax.
Hackle.—Short woolly blue feather from breast of blue bantam cock or hen, two or, at most, three turns.
Whisks.—Two fibres of brownish blue *un*speckled feather from neck of cock guinea-fowl undyed—short.
Rib.—Optional—yellow tying silk, gold wire, or none.
Body.—Hare's fleck or, for a paler pattern, hare's poll.

III. *Early May*

Hook.—No. 1 or even 2 down-eyed round bend.
Tying Silk.—Grey brown, waxed with colourless wax.
Hackle.—Light medium honey dun hen, short in fibre. Two turns.
Whisks.—Two strands pale-brownish blue cock guinea-fowl's neck—short.

Rib.—Fine silver wire or none.
Body.—*Abdomen*: Pale-brown peacock's quill, stripped.
    Thorax: Hare's poll.

IV. *June*

Hook.—No. 1 down-eyed round bend or No. 15 Pennell sneck.
Tying Silk.—Primrose, waxed with brown harness-maker's wax.
Hackle.—Dark-blue hen or cockerel.
Whisks.—Two strands of unspeckled pale-blue cock guinea-fowl's neck—short.
Rib.—Fine gold wire.
Body.—*Abdomen*: Raw lamb's wool mixed with brown olive seal's fur—just enough to shade it.
    Thorax: English squirrel's blue fur.

V. *May, June and July*

Hook.—No. 15 or 16 down-eyed Pennell sneck.
Tying Silk.—Purple or grey brown, waxed with dark wax.
Hackle.—Dark-blue dun hen or cockerel, to extend slightly beyond the dubbing of thorax.
Whisks.—Two strands of dark unspeckled neck feathers of cock guinea-fowl—tied very short.
Rib (optional).—Silver wire.
Body.—*Abdomen*: Strand of brown quill from the stalk of the eye feather of a peacock, stripped.
    Thorax: A wad of dark hare's ear, close up to the hackle.

VI. *June and July*

Hook.—No. 1 down-eyed round bend, or No. 15 or 16 down-eyed Pennell sneck.

Tying Silk.—Pale orange, waxed with clear colourless wax.

Hackle.—Darkish blue cockerel's hackle, one turn or, at most, two—very short.

Whisks.—Two strands of darkish unfreckled cock guinea-fowl's neck—short.

Body.—*Abdomen*: Three or four strands of pale covert feather of heron dyed in picric acid and wound from tail to shoulder.

Thorax: English blue squirrel's fur or, as a change, dark hare's ear.

A variety of shades of this pattern may be dressed by using darker or lighter heron's herl for the body. A very **deadly** fly on its day.

VII. *May and throughout season when small darkish Watery Dun is on*

Hook.—No. 16 down-eyed Pennell sneck.

Tying Silk.—Bright yellow, waxed with clear colourless wax.

Hackle.—Dark-blue hen short—not more than 2 turns.

Whisks.—Two strands darkish blue unspeckled feather from neck of cock guinea-fowl—short.

Body.—Thinly laid dubbing of mole's fur mixed with yellow seal's fur.

This pattern is adapted from John Younger's favourite pattern of olive dun. The body may be varied by using English squirrel blue fur instead of mole. It has proved in the one season during which I have tried it a very useful pattern.

VIII. *July and August*

Hook.—No. 15 down-eyed Pennell sneck.
Tying Silk.—Pale carrot colour, waxed with clear colourless wax, at shoulder only.
Hackle.—Brownish dun with paler points—short.
Whisks.—Two strands of pale-brownish blue unfreckled neck feather of cock guinea-fowl—short.
Body.—*Abdomen*: Pale-pinkish artificial silk tied in at shoulder and wound over its waste end and the whisk fibres and bare shank to near bend and then once under the whisks and back in successive turns to shoulder.
Thorax: Hare's poll.

This nymph when wet through goes a sort of honey brown translucent hue. Very deadly on its day. Its defect is that the silk is apt to tear with the trout's teeth and get fluffy.

July Dun

IX. *July and August*

Hook.—No. 17 down-eyed Pennell sneck.
Tying Silk.—Pale orange, waxed with colourless wax.
Hackle.—Rusty dun cock, very short in fibre—one turn.
Whisks.—Two strands cock guinea-fowl's neck feather dyed in picric acid and tied very short.
Rib.—Fine gold wire.
Body.—*Abdomen*: Medium blue fox fur, brightly dyed in picric acid.
Thorax: Dark-brownish olive seal's fur or some darkish dun fur as a variation.

Iron-blue Dun

X. Late April to end of July and a smaller Variety from mid-August to End of Season

Hook.—No. 15 Bartleets B 7362 or, if that cannot be had, No. 17 down-eyed Pennell sneck.
Tying Silk.—Crimson, waxed with colourless wax.
Hackle.—Shortest hackle from throat of cock jackdaw—one turn or, at most, two.
Whisks.—Three strands of soft white hen hackle—quite short.
Body.—Mole's fur spun thinly on the tying silk exposing two turns of silk at tail, tapering to thickest at shoulder. See also p. 104.

Pale Watery Duns

There are four varieties of Pale Watery of which three are common and some or other are on from mid-April to the end of the season and later. I have seen them hatching in bitter weather when fishing for grayling in December. These nymphs vary a great deal in colour and within limits in size.

XI. *April and May, and again in July and August*

Hook.—No. 15 Bartleets B 7362 or, failing that, No. 17 down-eyed Pennell sneck—short.
Tying Silk.—Primrose, waxed with colourless wax.
Hackle.—One turn of *very* small darkish blue cockerel.
Whisks.—Two strands pale unfreckled neck feather of cock guinea-fowl—short.
Rib.—Yellow silk—five turns.
Body.—English squirrel's blue fur laid on thinly at tail and tapered to thickest at shoulder.

XII

Same. Substituting fine silver wire for yellow silk rib.

XIII

Hook.—No. 1 down-eyed round bend, or No. 15 down-eyed Pennell sneck.
Silk.—White, waxed with colourless wax.
Hackle.—Honey dun cockerel, very short—one turn only.
Whisks.—Two strands of pale unfreckled neck feather of guinea-fowl—short.
Body.—Cream-coloured fur from belly of baby seal.
Thorax.—Blue squirrel or hare's fur.

XIV

Hook.—As No. 15 or 16, down-eyed Pennell sneck.
Tying Silk.—Yellow; at shoulder only.
Hackle.—Pale honey dun cock, very short—one turn.
Whisks.—Pale-brownish blue neck feather of cock guinea-fowl tied in at shoulder so as to be short beyond body when body material wound on.
Body.—*Abdomen*: One strand from three-ply yellow silk going greenish olive when wet, tied in at shoulder with the waste end towards the tail, wound over whisks and bare hook to tail them once under the whisk and back in taper to shoulder.
  Thorax: Hare's poll or, for variation, squirrel's blue fur.

XV. *May to August*

Hook.—No. 16 down-eyed Pennell sneck.

Tying Silk.—Crimson or hot orange for head and thorax; white for rest of body. Both waxed with colourless wax.
Hackle.—Pale-reddish centre with white points—quite short.
Whisks.—Two strands palest (but not white) neck feather of cock guinea-fowl—short.
Rib.—Fine silver wire.
Body.—*Abdomen*: Baby seal's fur—cream colour.
    Thorax: Rabbit's poll dyed in Red Ant dye.
A very useful pattern, where the nymphs which look as if they bled at the head are taken.

XVI

Hook.—No. 16 down-eyed Pennell sneck.
Tying Silk.—Cream, waxed with colourless wax.
Hackle.—Medium dun hen with pale points—one turn.
Whisks.—Two strands creamy neck feather of cock guinea-fowl.
Rib.—Fine silver wire.
Body.—*Abdomen*: Whitey grey fur from hare's shoulder.
    Thorax: Darker fur—in a variety of shades—from blue English squirrel or hare's fur. On its day a very deadly pattern.

XVII

Hook.—No. 16.
Tying Silk.—Cream, waxed with colourless wax.
Hackle.—Palest ginger hen—one turn—short.
Whisk.—Two strands of palest creamy neck feather of cock guinea-fowl—short.
Rib.—Fine silver wire.

Body.—*Abdomen*: Pale rabbit's poll.
> *Thorax*: Hare's poll, or, for a variation, English squirrel's blue fur.

Blue-winged Olive

XVIII

The nymph of this insect is sometimes, but not often, taken during the daytime—much oftener at night. Then (though why I have never been able even to surmise) a pattern dressed thus will sometimes be taken greedily.

Hook.—No. 1 or 2 down-eyed round bend.
Tying Silk.—Hot orange.
Hackle.—Dark but definitely blue hen—as woolly in the fibre as can be had—two turns.
Whisk.—Three strands of dark hen hackle—short.
Body.—Cow-hair the colour of dried blood, dressed fat—the nymph itself being fat and not taper like the other dun nymphs.

In the daytime I have occasionally had trout on an actual imitation of the nymph, using two shades of olive seal's fur to match the upper and lower parts of the insect. It is not possible to describe the exact shades.

I have also, when trout have been taking Blue-winged Olive nymphs during the daytime—a rather violent type of rise—had occasional success with a pattern dressed thus:

Hook.—No. 1 down-eyed round bend.
Tying Silk.—Ordinary orange.
Hackle.—Dark blue.
Whisk.—Three strands of close-freckled partridge hackle.
Body.—Fur of blue Persian cat strongly dyed in picric acid—becoming a rich green.

For grayling taking Blue-winged Olive nymphs in the daytime I have also used, with a measure of success, a pattern dressed as follows:

Hook.—No. 1 down-eyed round bend.
Tying Silk.—Orange.
Hackle.—Greenish olive cock.
Wing Cases.—Brownish-blue starling wing feather.
Whisks.—Three strands of partridge closely freckled brown hackle.
Rib.—Fine gold wire.
Body.—A mixture of a variety of seal's fur, olive and green and yellow with a hint of orange and red, all mixed with hare's poll and the green dyed fur above described—to make it spin easily—but I never found this pattern of any use for trout.

XVI

BIBLIOGRAPHICAL

It may be a matter of comment that in this short work I have made little or no reference to the work of other writers on the subject. The bibliography on the subject is small. Of the art in its present form little has been written. But necessarily there have been forerunners.

The Rev. Richard Durnford, whose *Diary of a Test Fisherman*, 1809 to 1819 (published in 1911 by Mr Henry Nicoll), I have mentioned before, showed himself well aware of the nymphing habits of the Test trout. For example, on page 6 of the volume he says: "Taken from the stomach of a trout, they are the nymphae of the gnats ascending through the water before they take wing". His fishing however was usually done in rough water with more than one fly, and no doubt partook a good deal of the nature of that "fishing the water" which is the root of the purist's objection to the wet fly (and the nymph).

In 1863 came Dr Cutcliffe's extremely clever little volume on Devonshire trouting, *Trout Fishing in Rapid Streams*. His patterns are all hackled patterns, rather bulky, and are dressed with sharp bright hackles which would make the flies dance in the waters of the tumbling streams he frequented. But he let fall at page 118 the observation:

> I find so much spoken about the natural fly and its imitation, but little about the insect before arrived at its maturity. How seldom does one imitate the larvae or pupae of the several insects! Many of them must [*sic*] necessarily be often washed into the

water and devoured by the trout; and if looked into these will be found more like the hackle flies I use than are any flies in their perfect state.

Francis Francis (1857) with his historic sentence: "The judicious and perfect application of dry, wet, and mid-water fly fishing stamps the finished fly fisher with the hall mark of efficiency". But a subsequent sentence shows that his wet fly fishing was also the "fishing the water" order. "As a rule rough weather is more favourable to a sunk or wet fly while bright and calm weather favours the dry one." And he doesn't seem to have been aware of the nymph.

F. M. Halford in *Dry Fly Fishing in Theory and Practice* (1889) states that it is easy enough (as in fact it is) to dress an excellent representation of the natural nymph—but as he expressly declares that it will be quite ineffective he can hardly be considered a forerunner.

I believe my own first timid experiments, first described in book form in *Minor Tactics of the Chalk Stream* (1910), come next in order of date, though I imagine Dr J. C. Mottram must have been working on the subject about the same date, for the *Field* of the 5th February, 1912, contained a longish article by him over the pen name "Jim Jam", illustrated with two patterns of nymphs, used apparently for fishing, down-stream and dragging, for bulgers. Subsequently, in his book *Fly Fishing: Some New Arts and Mysteries*, first published in 1915, he had, under the chapter-heading "Nymphs and Bulgers", an eloquent and, I thought and think, convincing exposition of the then new school of Nymph Fishing. I gather from a recent paper of his in the *Fly Fishers' Club Journal* that he has recanted, and I am sorry—for him.

The next book dealing with the subject was *The Way of a Trout with a Fly* (1921), in which two methods of dressing

BIBLIOGRAPHICAL

more precise and detailed representations of the nymph are described and illustrated.

Henry Nicoll who, as before stated, published *The Diary of a Test Fisherman* (the Rev. Richard Durnford, 1809 to 1819) in 1911, published another volume in 1923 called *Salmon and Other Things*, on page 53 of which he writes:

> On some days the trout will not take surface flies, and your beautiful little dun may float down without being regarded by fish either small or great. On such days trout may be taken by fishing just under the surface of the water, and perhaps this method affords the most enchanting sport the chalk stream yields.
>
> A hot sunny day is to be desired. The fisherman wanders slowly up the river until a fish of a worthy size is spotted. The fish must look intelligent and be taking notice. If he is watched it will be seen that he opens and shuts his mouth from time to time in the act of feeding. He does not take any floating duns which may come down, occasionally he just breaks the surface of the water, but it is not often.
>
> Then the angler looks out his under-water flies which range from a fat black alder, or a Coch-y-bonddu, down the scale to small things of hackle and fluff. Whatever the choice of fly may be, it is wetted in the mouth or in the river and lightly dropped a few inches in front of the fish. If all goes well you can almost hear the fish say, "Here is a fat drowned alder, or a delicious little beetle, etc." Then you see the fish's mouth shut and the moment to strike has come.

At the time this was written nymph fishing had not become at all a common practice. Mr Henry Nicoll's own water was the Bullingdon tributary of the Test at and below Sutton Scotney.

Mr Eric Taverner's first work, *Divers Ways to Tackle Trout* (1925), is silent on the use of the artificial nymph, but his monumental *Trout Fishing from all Angles* (1929) had a good deal to say about the artificial nymph, its dressing and methods of fishing it—not only in chalk streams but in other waters—and he treats the claim of the artificial nymph as established and the battle for it as won.

So again does Colonel E. W. Harding in his *The Fly Fisher and the Trout's Point of View* (1931).

In Horace Hutchinson's *A Fellowship of Anglers* (1928) he recounts how the late Henry Birkbeck fished the Houghton Club water on the Test and fished successfully with flies tied by E. J. Power which "had a nymphish look to them". He also says of another member of the Club, Peter Haig Thomas, that "he was a great exponent of the 'brown nymph' and used it with deadly effect". Mr Thomas joined the Club in 1917 and retired in 1922. The book states that Henry Birkbeck "would often moisten one of his spiders to make it sink before coming to the fish".

Major John Waller Hills, P.C., M.P., devoted a chapter of the Second (enlarged) Edition of *A Summer on the Test*, published in 1930, to "The Nymph". I take the liberty to quote from page 243 a trio of sentences:

More and more each year does nymph fishing become a part of the modern angler's equipment, and he who does not possess the art is gravely handicapped. At the same time has come the realisation that this art is both difficult and delightful. It demands different qualities and it makes a different appeal, it opens a new field of observation and experiment, and it is as exacting a process as the other, for upon my word I find trout harder to catch under water than on top.

Major Hills' testimony is valuable, inasmuch as he was brought up on a difficult North Country river where the practice is to fish up-stream wet.

His subsequent book, *My Sporting Life*, published in 1934, devotes some pages to the art of nymph fishing. He says, "This is not only legitimate fly fishing but fly fishing of a high order, harder than the floating fly".

He had previously referred to the use of the nymph in his

BIBLIOGRAPHICAL

History of Fly Fishing for Trout (1921), where he describes it as "being built on new lines copying more closely the original". He adds: "These are now being used extensively and with success in the shyest chalk streams".

The next work dealing with the subject to which I need refer is my third volume, *Side Lines, Side Lights and Reflections* (1932), containing at pages 244-246 a description of my simplified method of dressing nymphs much as here expounded though in less detail—and the prescriptions of eleven of my more attractive patterns repeated from the autumn, 1931, number of the *Journal* of the Fly Fishers' Club.

Mr R. D'Oyley Hemingway (Hafren), in *Fly Fishing for Trout*, published in 1935, has a brief reference to nymph fishing; but, after saying that imitation nymphs are made which are fished with dry-fly action, but with the nymph sunken more or less, goes on, "Purposely I say no more about it, for nymph fishing is not for the beginner".

Mr Roger Woolley, professional fly-dresser and tackle dealer (who has the somewhat exceptional qualification in his line of business of knowing something of anglers' entomology and of making a genuine endeavour to produce accurate representations of insects), published in 1932 a volume on fly-dressing called *Modern Trout Fly Dressing*, and in this he gave dressings of a number of nymphs of the Ephemeridae, but did not deal with methods of nymph fishing as an art or with its ethics.

Mr T. J. Hanna in his book, *Fly Fishing in Ireland*, published in 1933, pays nymph fishing the compliment of devoting his first chapter of seventeen pages to it—and he takes the occasion to protest against "the monstrous creatures offered as nymphs by some tackle dealers". He himself does not belong to that class. The chapter deserves attentive reading, though I do not agree with all of it. In addition he gives later on some examples of his methods of dressing nymphs.

C. Ernest Pain in *Fifty Years on the Test* (1934) has a chapter, "Of Flies Good and Bad", in which he discusses cases of fish nymphing and bulging and recognises some of the nymphs now in use as looking very attractive, but makes no pronouncements on the legitimacy or otherwise of nymph fishing on chalk streams. He does not seem to distinguish between casting the nymph to selected fish in position feeding subaqueously and the "chuck-and-chance-it" method of fishing the water. Nor does he make it clear that he realises that fish in position are often taking the mature nymph as it rises to hatch and letting the hatched subimago go by.

Another writer—Pat Castle—whose book, *Descriptive Angling*, also came out in 1935, devotes two chapters to nymph fishing, but as he uses the term nymph in so catholic a spirit as to include the Red and Black Palmer, a black water-beetle and several other beetles, I can hardly quote him as writing of the nymph in the way in which I, and I hope many chalk stream anglers, understand it.

Captain Robert Hartman in his book *About Fishing*, also published in 1935, discusses nymph fishing at pages 254 and 255. He says:

To the dispassionate angler there is nothing reprehensible about catching a chalk stream trout on a nymph. The nymph is not a magician, it is not a deadly lure that will denude the river of fish. In point of fact it is less killing than the dry fly, but it has the merit of catching fish which are not in the mood to take the fly on the surface. Considered ethically there can be no difference between fishing with an artificial ephemera designed to represent the insect a minute before it becomes a dun and fishing with one which represents the same insect a minute after it has ceased to be a nymph. Both are representational forms of ephemera fishing and if one of them is fair play, so, also, must be the other.

BIBLIOGRAPHICAL

This volume contains instruction for dressing two types of nymph, which he appears to consider sufficient for all purposes. This would not be enough for the Itchen.

There are probably no two rivers, chalk stream or otherwise, where the conditions are exactly alike, indeed they vary from length to length of the same river. So one may find the trout behaving very differently, on one part being much given to nymphing, on another much more generally taking the fly on the surface.

On the stretch of the Itchen at Itchen Stoke I have seen the trout pegging away gaily at the floating fly, while two or three miles down they have been busy nymphing and letting the subimago go by.

In 1935 Lancelot Peart published a book called *South Country Fishermen*, written strictly from the dry-fly point of view by a man residing on the banks of a chalk stream (I imagine the Kennet) and able, therefore, to get on to the water at all times whenever conditions were attractive. While admitting that the use of the nymph has had a great deal of success he holds that

> to preserve a dry-fly stream entirely at its best, no under-water fishing whatever should be permitted. It reeks too much of hypnotism and over-solicitation. One may admittedly get more fish by adopting the principle of a method for a moment, and by repeatedly ringing the changes in one's technique.

But he is convinced that the ultimate result of such procedure is no less calamitous than a falling off of rising fish. They get no rest. Whether feeding on the surface or subaqueously they never can be free from care. There is always the need for vigilance if the cold cruel steel is not to be an affair of bitter experience rather than an unpleasant possibility.

I am doubtful, however, whether this author realises how

often the nymphing fish in position is hammered by dry-fly purists because he seems to be rising.

Mr L. R. Peart in a recent book, *Fishing in the Making: The Management of Chalk Streams*, has a few words on nymph fishing, and, while paying a tribute to the skill and pleasure involved, says:

> it takes a very good water to stand up indefinitely to nymph-fishing or up-stream fishing with the wet fly. On a hard-fished water trout get no rest at all. Someone is for ever hammering at them with a wet fly or nymph. *Nymph fished during a rise is a different matter altogether.* But few men with a nymph on their cast can resist a throw at every trout they see *whether he is feeding or not.* Extremely wary trout are the inevitable results.

The italics are mine. With every due respect to Mr Peart this is unmitigated nonsense. No angler who had the most elementary knowledge of his job would cast a nymph to a fish that is not feeding—either obviously coming to the surface or hovering to take the insect life brought to him. At any other time he is either hugging the bottom or hidden in the weeds.

I quote also from the same work from a chapter, "The Problem of the Fishing Club," two suggested rules which are relevant:

> (1) No down-stream wet-fly fishing to be done whatever. It is certain to result in trout being shy.
>
> (2) Nowadays, educated up to the art by such men as Mr G. E. M. Skues, many anglers use up-stream wet flies and nymphs. I am well aware that there is no little skill in these methods and much pleasure to be derived from it. In my opinion, however, it takes a very good water to stand up indefinitely to nymph fishing or up-stream fishing with the wet fly. When these practices are abused, as they very frequently are, the quality of the fishing is bound to fall off. On a hard-fished water trout get no rest at all. Someone is for ever hammering at them with a wet fly or a nymph. *Nymph fished during a rise is a different matter altogether.* But few men with a nymph on their cast can resist a throw at every trout they

see whether he is feeding or not. Extremely wary trout are the inevitable result. Thus, before permitting methods of this kind, I would always put the matter to the vote and abide by the decision of the majority of those fishing the water.

A wet fly may be permitted in such places as hatch-holes and weir-pools. The stock of trout in such places is apt to be heavy compared with other parts of the river, while there, too, will be found old fish which are better out of the water. Big fancy flies, however, should be prohibited. So should sink-and-draw methods.

The italics are mine. According to my experience it is of little use to cast a nymph to a trout that is not feeding. If he is in position to feed, he is invariably feeding.

Major R. C. Simpson in *Fish and Find Out* (1937) has a chapter on "Nymphing and Notes on Wading" in which he likens nymph fishing to up-stream worm fishing in rough rivers. It is therefore not entirely in point in relation to nymph fishing on chalk streams, for the nymphs are cast (although up-stream) at large to search the water and not to individual fish in position.

There are of course many writers who assume that the sort of hackled wet fly used on rough streams is taken for a nymph. That is not my opinion. I think flies of that type are taken for flies caught and tumbled in the very act of emerging from the nymph stage, and only for the complete nymph if fished dragging. I do not therefore think that any further reference to such writers is required in this chapter, nor to such as deliberately describe long-hackled patterns as nymphs.

The latest book dealing with the subject (up to the date of this going to the printers) is W. Carter Platts's *Modern Trout Fishing*, which has an open-minded and appreciative chapter on Nymph Fishing, though I could wish that he had realised the distinction between nymphing trout which are bulging and trout which are taking the mature nymphs quietly and methodically under banks and in runs.

INDEX

Abbots' Barton, 53
About Fishing (Capt. Robert Hartman), 124
Acceptance of nymph, 43
Accuracy, 15
Act of emerging, 25
Active nymph, and activity of, 17, 18, 19, 20, 22, 23, 24, 25, 26, 42, 73, 74, 75, 78
Addition to technique, 57
Advance in art of fly fishing, 82
Adverse breeze inimical, 44
Alder, the, 33, 54
Alexandra, 10, 11
Alleged nymphs, 12
American light rods, 55
Angler's Vade-Mecum (Pulman), 4
Angling Press, 12
Anton (river), 63
Apologia, 1, 2
Art, nymph fishing a branch of chalk stream angler's, 2
a difficult, 122
old, of wet fly on chalk streams, 14
Artificial nymph, 9, 10, 12, 13, 22, 26, 34, 35, 37, 40, 41, 42, 43, 46, 57, 66, 73, 121, 122
attractive to trout, 74
of Mayfly, 48
Artificial silk, 100
Ascending nymph, 4, 18, 20, 22, 23, 36, 74, 78
"Assorted Rises", 31, 32
Attraction for subaqueously feeding trout, 74
Austin, R. S., 52, 55
Autobiography, An Angler's (Halford), 67
Autopsy, 2, 7, 15, 21, 54, 57, 75, 77, 78
Avoidance of undersized fish, 15

Baby plate, 8, 29, 57, 58, 97, 104, 107
advantages of, 29
Baby seals' fur, 100

Backwaters, 43
Badminton Library, 5, 83
Bartleets absorbed by Milwards, 91
Bartleets hooks (B 7362), 91
Bavaria, 54
Bays and eddies, 42-47
Beetles, 9, 10, 12
water, 33
Best chance of taking nymphing trout, 19, 36
Bibliographical, 119-127
Birkbeck, Henry, 122
Blackbird hen, hackles, 94
Bloody Butcher, 9-10
Blow line, 5
Blue Upright, 98
Blue-winged olive nymph, 44, 55, 75, 94, 97
Bob fly, 4, 67
Bodies of nymphs, 97
Bona fide rises, 74
Bosnian streams, 55
Bottom food, 21
Bouglé, Louis, 55, 56
Branchiae, 11, 101
Breathing processes, 11, 101
Breeze, adverse, inimical, 44
strong, 3
Brown nymph, 122
Bulgers or bulging trout, 6, 7, 16, 17, 18, 19, 20, 35, 36, 53, 70, 71, 72, 73, 74, 75, 76, 77, 78, 83, 87, 88, 120, 124
Bulging at Mayfly nymph, 48
Bullingdon River (Test tributary), 121
Buxton, Lord, 83

Caddis flies, 32
Caperer, 4
Carlisle, Major (South West), 67
Cast, sinking of, 34; to steady the, 4, 67
Casting, at random, 10
delicacy of, 34
direction of, 34

Casting—*contd.*
  nymph, 27-28
Castle, Pat (*Descriptive Angling*), 124
Casual feeder, 38
Cellire, 100
Celluloid varnish, 105
"Chuck and chance it", 69, 124
Claims for nymph-fishing, 82
Claret spinner, 50
Clay, use of moist, 35
Coggeshall, W. D., 55
Colne (river), 52
Colours of tying silks, 102, 106
Conditions favourable to dry fly, 70-80
  favourable to wet fly, 70-71
Contents of trout's stomach, 2, 8, 10, 11, 20, 23 (note), 28, 29, 40, 54, 57, 75-77, 86, 99, 104, 107
Coquet (river), 52
Cotton, 3
Cox, Irwin E. B., 51, 52, 53, 77
Cross line, 4, 5
Cruising trout, 40, 41, 44
Cutcliffe, Dr, 52, 119

Dark effect of nymphs, 98
Deadly, said to be too, 85
Debate at Fly Fishers' Club, 68, 89
Definition of nymph, 9
Definition, of nymph fishing, 13
  of trout in position, 16
Delicacy of presentation, 34
Demons, 10
Depths (middle and lower) of water, 77
Derbyshire Derwent, 54
Descriptive Angling (Pat Castle), 124
Despotism of dry fly, 10
Devon Blue Upright, quill for, 98
Diary of a Test Fisherman (Durnford), 3, 4, 63, 67, 119, 121
  patterns of flies in, 4
"Dimpling" trout rise, 19, 47
Direction of casting, 34
Disbelief of Halford, 68, 69, 71, 72, 75, 79, 81
Distended shuck of nymph, 21, 23, 26
Divers Ways to tackle Trout (Taverner), 32
Dominance of dry fly, 3, 5, 14, 63, 65

Double-hooked Greenwell's Glory, 53
Down-stream fishing, 4, 5
Down-stream flailer, 67
Down-stream flogging or flogger, 68, 71, 72, 80, 81
Drag, 3, 34, 37, 41, 42, 44, 45, 47, 62, 69, 85
Dragging fly, 6, 10, 36, 45, 47, 48, 67, 75, 77, 81, 82, 95, 120
Draw, the, 43
Dressing nymphs, 8, 11, 12, 57, 59, 73, 74, 76, 97-107, 124
Dry fly, 3, 4, 5, 6, 7, 14, 34, 53, 68, 71, 83, 85
  fanatics, 10
  fishing, 6, 20, 34, 35, 67, 82; a religion, 5, 14; correct practice left intact, 82
  purism, 1, 31, 62, 64
  rods, heavy and powerful, 6, 23, 67
Dry Fly Fishing in Theory and Practice (Halford), 5, 20, 22, 24, 52, 67, 68, 72, 73, 74, 75, 76, 77, 78, 80, 81, 120
Dry Fly Man's Handbook, 16, 66, 67, 69, 71, 76, 80-81
Dubbing, 98
  pad of, for wing cases, 93
Durnford, Rev. Richard, 3, 4, 63, 67, 71, 119, 121; his patterns, 4
Dyed gut for bodies, 100
Dyed horsehair for bodies, 100
Dyes, 100

Effects (alleged) of fishing nymph, 63
Entry, good, 4, 53, 95
Ephemeridae or Ephemeroptera, 2, 9, 10, 25, 32, 34, 123
Ethics, 14, 75, 76, 85, 87, 88, 123
Evolution of nymph fishing, 3-8
Exact representation, 13, 28, 29, 99
Exact reproduction, 58
"Exact wet-fly fishing", 82
Exceptions, 49-50
Extraction of contents of trout's stomach, 7
Eyed hooks for floating flies, 4

Fanatics, dry fly, 10
Fancy flies, 9, 10, 127
Fancy patterns, 46

130

INDEX

Feeding habits of trout to be studied, 31
Fellowship, A, of Anglers (Hutchinson), 122
"Fiasco", 79
Field, the, 4, 51, 54, 56, 120
Fifty Years on the Test (C. E. Pain), 124
Finish, close to eye of hook, 102
two half hitches, 102
whip, 102
Fish and Find Out (Major R. C. Simpson), 127
Fisher, Major (Rod and River), 83
Fisheries Exhibition, 1883, 51
Fishing Club, problem of the, 126-127
Fishing Gazette, 52, 56
Fishing in the Making (L. R. Peart), 126
Fishing the nymph, 31-48
Fishing the rise, 68
Fishing the water, 15, 47, 66, 68, 81, 119, 120, 124
Fishing with the wind, 5
Flailer, down-stream, 67, 68
"Flies Good and Bad" (C. E. Pain), 124
Flies, winged, in the 'seventies, 4
salmon, 10, 12
sea-trout, 10, 12
Floating Flies and how to Dress Them (Halford), 5, 51, 83
"Floating Flies and Sunk Flies" (Halford), 68
Floating fly, 4, 5, 6, 7, 13, 14, 19, 21, 22, 37, 45, 51, 62, 68, 70, 125
Floating nymph, 19, 20, 75
Floggers (or flogging) of the water, 6, 68, 71, 72, 79, 80
Floss-silk for bodies, 85, 100, 106
Fly Casting Tournament, 1904, 55
Fly, dragging, 6, 10, 36, 47, 67, 75, 77
Flyfisher, The, and the Trout's Point of View (Col. Harding), 7, 38, 39, 78, 122
Fly Fishers' Club, 13, 53, 68
Fly Fishers' Club Journal, 31, 56, 120, 123
Fly Fishing for Trout (Hemingway), 123

Fly Fishing in Ireland (Hanna), 123
Fly fishing, nymph fishing said not to be, 87
Fly Fishing: Some New Arts and Mysteries (Mottram), 17, 36, 120
Fly rods, Leonard, 86
Foster, David, 83
Fox fur, 100
Francis Francis, 4, 5, 51, 77, 120
Frequency of rise, 41
Frome, Dorsetshire, 5
Fur, translucent, 98
Furs for bodies, 99-100

Gallena for whisks, 104
Gap, nymph fishing fills a, 82
Gaze, upward, of trout, 39, 78
Gear, rods and, 27-29
Glycerine, use of, 35
Gnats, 33
Godwin, Alfred, 53
Gold-ribbed Hare's Ear, 49-50
Gold wire, 99, 101
Good entry, 4, 53, 95
Goose herl, 100
Gossamer gut, 52
Grannom, 33
Greenwell's Glory (small double-hooked), 53, 54
Grey, Viscount, 83
Grizzly King, 9
Gut (dyed), for bodies, 100

Hackles for nymphs, 41, 93-95, 102
Hafren (R. D'O. Hemingway), 123
Halford, F. M., 4, 5, 6, 13, 14, 15, 16, 20, 22, 24, 25, 40, 46, 49, 53, 57, 58
misapprehensions of, see Misapprehensions
pronouncements of, 15, 22, 26, 40, 53, 57, 65-83, 75, 89, 97, 120
Hall, H. S., and eyed hook, 4-5
and dry fly, 83
Hammering nymphing trout, 14, 75, 86, 87, 126
Hammond, John, 5, 53
Hanna, T. J., 11, 123
Harding, Col. E. W., 33, 38, 39, 78, 83, 122
Hare's fur, 100
Hare's poll, 99

Hartman, Capt. Robert, 124
Hawker, Col. Peter, 4
Head and tail rise, 41, 47
Heavy lines, 6
Hemingway, R. D'O., 123
Heretics, 14, 15
Herl, 100
Heron herl, 100
Hills, Major John Waller, 122, 123
Historical development of nymph fishing, 3-8
History of nymph fishing, 4-8
History of Fly Fishing for Trout (Major John Waller Hills), 123
Hodgson, Earl, 83
Holland, George, 49, 52
Hook, eyed (H. S. Hall), 4
Hooks, 91-92
Horsehair dyed for bodies, 100
Houghton Club, 5, 67, 122
Hovering trout, 19, 126
Hutchinson, Horace (*A Fellowship of Anglers*), 122

Ignorance of nymphs among anglers, 6, 13, 15, 62, 65
Illegitimate patterns or lures, 10, 62, 65
  practices, 81
Imitating nymphs, 22, 57, 73, 74, 76, 97
Imitation of Mayfly numph, 48
Immature nymph, 20, 24, 73
Inactive nymph, *see* Inert nymph
India-rubber for bodies, 101
Individual fish, 6, 14, 15, 19, 42, 48, 56, 66, 67, 68, 80, 81
Inert nymph, 17, 19, 20, 22, 23, 24, 25, 26, 37, 39, 42, 45, 74, 76, 78
Inertia, periods of, 25
Innovation, nymph fishing an, 34
Insect food of trout, 32-33
Instinct, 44
Intolerance, 65
Itchen (river), 4, 5, 11, 33, 40, 51, 52, 53, 58, 59, 77, 79
Itchen Stoke, 125

"Jim Jam" (Dr. Mottram), 120

Kennet (river), 33, 48, 54. 125

Lakes, 94
Landrail hackle, 94
Larvae, 9, 15, 21, 73, 74, 77
  frequently imitated, 79
Larval stages of Ephemeroptera, 2, 17, 21, 34
Legitimate fly fishing, nymph fishing, 122
  nymph fishing, 48, 81
  use of term nymphs, 2
Leonard fly rods, 55
Light rods, 55, 68
Limerick hooks, unsuitability for nymphs, 91
Limit of numbers, 35
Lines, heavy tapered oil silk, 6, 67
Lining trout, 45, 46
Live nymph in mouth of trout, 23
Looking downward, trout not, 78
Lures, 2, 9, 10, 12, 45, 46, 62, 63, 65

Mallard, breast feather dyed, 94
Management of Chalk Streams (L. R. Peart), 126
Manifold (river), 54
March Brown, 97
Marrow scoop or spoon, 2, 8, 28, 29, 57, 58, 104
Marryat, George Selwyn, 5, 14, 22, 76, 77
Mature nymph, 17, 19, 20, 22, 23, 24, 37, 57, 71, 73, 77, 80
Materials (body) to take up water, 35, 41
Mayfly, 24, 48, 75
Mayfly nymph, 24, 48
Medium Olive Dun of spring, 49
Method of using marrow scoop, 28
Methods of tying nymphs, 103, 104, 105
Midge, 38
Mills, Thomas Bates, of New York, 55
Milwards (absorb Bartleets), 91
Minor Tactics of the Chalk Stream, 7, 15, 47, 56, 57, 58, 120
Mirror, 38, 39, 46, 47, 78
Misapprehensions of Halford, 58, 66, 70-75, 78, 80
Missel thrush hackles, 94
Modern angler's equipment, 122
Modern Trout Fly Dressing (Woolley), 123

INDEX

Monstrosities, 12, 34, 123
Mosely, Martin E., 4, 13, 20, 25, 26
Motionless nymphs, 19, 22, 23, 76
Motion of nymph, 18, 74
Mottram, Dr, 17, 18, 19, 22, 23, 36, 63, 74, 83, 120
   his nymph patterns, 120
Mud, use of river, to sink gut, 35

Nicoll, Henry, 3, 67, 119, 121
Nicolls, Rev. E. R. J., 77
Normandy chalk streams, 55
North Country angler (Reffitt), 69
   angler (another), 79, 94
   hackles, 10
   patterns, 7, 78
   streams, 47, 71
   wet-fly fishing, 68
Norwegian waters, 55, 56
Number limit, 35
Nymph, abdomina of, 98
   acceptance of, 43
   action, 17, 18, 19, 20, 23, 24, 25, 42
   alleged, 12
   approaching, reflection in mirror, 39, 46, 78
   artificial, 9, 10, 13, 14, 22-26, 34, 35, 37, 41, 42, 43, 46, 57, 66, 73, 121, 122; of Mayfly, 24, 48, 76; like winged fly of the 'seventies, 4
   ascending, 4, 20, 22, 23, 38, 45, 74, 124
   attraction of artificial, 74
   blue-winged olive, 55, 117-118
   brown, 122
   definition of, 9
   dimpling, 19, 47
   dragging, 18, 120
   floating, 19, 21, 22, 75
   hatching, 7, 22
   ignorance of angler, 6, 15
   ignorance of tackle dealers, *see* tackle dealers
   imitating, 22, 57, 73, 76, 97
   immature, 20, 24, 73
   in act of hatching, 7, violent undulations of abdomen, 25
   in mouth of trout, 7, 23, 52
   inert, 17, 19, 22, 23, 24, 25, 26, 32, 37, 39, 42, 74, 76, 78
   legitimate term, 2

Nymph—*contd.*
   live in mouth of trout, 23
   mature, 17, 18, 19, 20, 22, 24, 25, 37, 71, 77, 80, 124
   motionless, 19, 22, 23
   natural, 1, 9, 10, 11, 12, 22, 25, 26, 35, 36, 37, 42, 45, 46, 67, 97, 98
   olive, 56
   outline of, 97
   patterns, simple, 105
   presentation of, 34
   shape of, 9
   swimming, 18, 19, 25, 53
   taper of, 97
   way of a trout with a, 17-26
   wriggle of, 22, 23, 73
"Nymph, The" (Major J. W. Hills), 122
"Nymphae of gnats" (Durnford), 4, 119
Nymphal patterns, 7, 109-118
Nymph fishing, addition to technique, 57
   alleged effects, 63
   a new art, 14, 83
   auxiliary sport, 13
   beyond many anglers, 82, 85, 86
   branch of chalk stream angler's art, 2
   case for, 65
   definition of, 13
   during rise, 126 (twice)
   evolution of, 3-8
   fills a gap, 14, 82
   harder than floating fly, 122
   history of, 3-8
   innovation, 34
   justification of, 2
   legitimate, 12
   new phase of old art, 14
   not easier than dry fly, 62, 83
   not exclusive method, 13, 31
   not for beginners, 122
   on Usk, 15, 58, 59
   one phase of chalk stream fishing, 27
   said not to be fly fishing, 87
   said to be too deadly, 85
   special difficulties, 62
   still much misunderstood, 34
   true and proper practice, 2
   true art of, 10

"Nymphing and Notes on Wading"
  (Major R. C. Simpson), 127
Nymphing trout, 7, 34, 49, 75, 124
  best chances of taking, 36
  not looking downward, 78
  see Hammering
Nymphing under banks or in runs, 19,
  20, 22, 23, 24, 25, 35, 36, 43, 44,
  46, 54, 74, 88
"Nymphs and Bulgers" (Dr Mottram), 120
Nymphs, bodies of, 97, 98
  colour of, 94
  dressing methods, 57, 59, 76, 97-107
  exact representation of, 13, 28, 29
  floss bodies, 106
  hackles for, 41, 93-95
  hooks for, 91-92
  imitation of, 57, 73, 76, 97
  in bays and eddies, 42, 47
  in strong current, 41
  in tank, 25
  migration of, 35
  observation of, 28
  patterns of, 7, 109-118
  proportion of, in trout's stomach, large, 8
  representation of, *see* Representation
  short hackled patterns, 7
  stream of, 37
  taper of bodies, 98
  thorax of, 98
  trout feeding on, *passim*
  winged flies and, 2

Oiled cast, 42
Oiled silk lines, 6
Old art of wet fly, 14
Old Barge River, Winchester, 51, 53
Olive nymph, 56
Onion skin in vinegar (dye), 100
Opossum (fur), 100
Overton, 58

Pain, C. E., 124
Partridge hackle, 94
Patterns of nymphs, 7, 109-118
  not standard, 109
Peacock's tail, 101
  wing feather, 101-102
Peart, Lancelot, 125

Peart, L. R., 125
Pennell, down-eyed sneck bend hooks, 91-92
Pentelow, F. S. K., 20
Perlidae, 33
Personal, 51-59
Phase, one, of chalk stream fishing, 27
Pheasant tail, 38
Phryganidae, 32
"Picking it off", 41-42
Picric acid, 100, 101
Pink Wickham, 50, 52
Platts, W. Carter, 127
Pope's Green Nondescript, 49-50
Pope, W. H., 49
Porpoise roll, 41, 47
Position, trout in, *see* Trout in position
Power, E. J., 122
Practical Angler (Stewart's), 83
Pre-dry-fly practice of wet fly, 3, 63, 67
Precision, 13, 34, 37, 57, 66, 72, 99
Presentation of nymph, 34, 37, 57
"Problem of the Fishing Club"
  (L. R. Peart), 126
Professor, the, 9
Pronouncements of Halford, *see* Halford Pronouncements
Proportion of fish hooked and lost on Mayfly nymph, 15, 76, 77
Pros and cons, 85-89
Pryce-Tannatt down-eyed round bend hooks, 91
Pulman, G. P. R., *Angler's Vade-Mecum*, 4
Purism and purists, dry fly, 1, 31, 36, 62, 65, 66, 76, 81, 82, 89

Quills for nymph bodies, 98, 101, 102

Rate of taking, 40
Reaction, 61-63
Red Quill, 49-50
Red Sedge, 38, 50
Red spinner (Tup's Indispensable), 55
Reffitt, Mr, on Upper Test, 69-70
Reflections in mirror of approaching nymph, 39, 46, 78
Representation, 8, 11, 12, 13, 29, 46, 67, 73, 87, 103, 104, 120, 121
Reproduction (exact) of nymph, 29, 34, 58

INDEX

Revolt, 2
Revolutioning Hampshire trout fishing, 79, 82
Rhithrogena semicolorata, 97
Rise, dimpling, 19, 47
  fishing the, 68
  forms, 31, 32, 35, 42
  head and tail, 41, 47
Rises, *bona fide*, 74
River Management (Pentelow and others), 22
Rod and line, dry-fly fishing, 27
  for nymph fishing, 27
Rod and River (Major Fisher), 83
Rod, old type of, long and soft, 53
Rods, and gear, 27-29
  light, 55, 68
  split cane, heavy and powerful, 6, 67
Rough days, 4, 5, 67
Rough water, 72, 87, 93, 94, 119
Ruffle, 45, 46, 87
Rules for waters (Peart), 126-127

Saliva, use of, 35
Salmon and Other Things (Nicoll), 121
Salmon flies, 10, 12
Scientific Angler, The (David Foster), 83
Searching the water, 5, 7, 10, 16, 66, 67, 81
Sea trout flies, 10, 12
Seal's fur, 98
Sedge flies, 32
Segmentation of bodies, 101
Selected individual fish in position, 19, 48, 66, 67, 80, 81, 124
Senior, William, 51, 53, 79
Setae, 9, 10, 21
Sheringham, H. T., 54, 56, 82
Side Lines, Side Lights and Reflections, 54, 123
Signs of trout taking nymph, 43-45
Silks, tying, 105-106
Simpson, Major, R. C., 127
Sinking of cast, 34, 41, 48, 56
Sizable trout, 35, 42
Sizes of hooks, 91-92
Skill, comparative, 81, 82, 126
Smooth waters, 39, 40, 45, 46, 82
Smuts, 33
South Country Fishermen (Peart), 125

South Esk, 51, 52
"South West" (Major Carlisle), 67
Spider patterns, 94
Spinner, claret, 50
Spinner-fall, 47
Spinners, spent, 38, 39, 40, 41, 47
Split-cane rods, 8
Spotting the rise, 68
Squirrel's fur, English blue, 100
Standards, nymphal patterns not, 11, 109
Stewart, *Practical Angler*, 83
Still days, weather or water, 38, 67, 68, 80, 87
Stone flies, 53
Stream of insects, 38
Suck, or sucking rise, 38, 47
"Sufficient" wind, 3, 67
Summer on the Test (Major J. W. Hills), 122
Sutton Scotney, 121
Swimming nymph, 18, 19, 25, 50, 53
Switch cast, 41

Tackle dealers' patterns, 2, 11, 34, 57, 62, 65, 123
Tailing trout, 17, 23, 35, 50
Tapered oil silk lines, 6
Taper of nymphs, 11, 96
Taverner, Eric, *Divers Ways to tackle Trout*, 32, 49; "Rise Forms", 32
Trout Fishing from All Angles, 32, 121
Tendency of trout to nymph, growing, 86
Test (river), 4, 57, 58, 59, 63, 67, 69, 70, 79, 119, 121, 122
Thames, 51
Thomas, Peter Haig, 122
Thorax of nymph, 98
Thorax of nymph opaque, 106
Thrush hackles, 94
Time of the take, 47
Tod, Ewen M., 54, 83
Translucency of fur and wool, 98
  of nymphal abdomen, 11, 98, 100
Transparency, 21
Trout, cruising, 40-41
  dimpling, 19, 47
  feeding on nymphs, 7
  hovering, 19

Trout—*contd.*
 in position, 16, 22, 27, 34, 41, 44, 45, 66, 81, 124, 125, 126
 insect food of, 32-33
 nymphing quietly under banks, etc., 19, 20, 23, 24, 25, 35, 36, 43, 44, 46, 54, 74, 77, 88
 stomach contents of, 2, 8, 10, 11, 20, 23 (note), 28, 29, 40, 54, 57, 75, 77, 86, 104, 107
 unsatisfied, 37
 upward gaze of, 39, 78
Trout Fishing from All Angles (Taverner), 32, 121
Trout Fishing in Rapid Streams (Cutcliffe), 52, 119
Tup's Indispensable, 36, 38, 55, 56
Tying silk for bodies, 106
Tying silk, not to show, 101
Tweed (river), 51-52, 53

Under colour of nymph to be imitated, 99, 105
Undersized fish, 10, 15, 16, 35, 36, 42, 48, 66, 80, 81
 avoidance of, 15
 catching, pricking or searing, 10, 16, 66
Unsatisfied trout, 37
Unselfishness of Halford's doctrines, 65
Unsizable fish, *see* Undersized
Upward gaze of trout, 39
Usk, nymph fishing on, 15, 58-59, 92, 109

Varnish, celluloid, 102, 105

Wandle River, 5, 67
Waste ends of floss silk, 106
Water beetles, 33
Water, fishing the, 15, 47, 66, 68, 81, 119, 120, 124
 searching the, 7, 10, 16, 66, 67, 81

Way of a Trout with a Fly, The, 32, 41, 57, 58, 102, 120
"Way of a Trout with a Nymph", 17-26
Weaver's beams, 56
Weed-cutting, 42
Wet fly, 5
Wet-fly fishing, 33, 35, 52, 68, 70, 71
 old art of, 3, 14
 on chalk streams, 1, 4, 6, 7, 13, 14, 34, 66, 67, 68, 71
 down-stream, 4
 up-stream, 6, 7, 44, 66, 67, 68
"Wet-fly fishing, exact", 82
Whip finish, 102, 103, 105
Whisks, 11, 102, 106
 to be kept short, 102
"Whistling wind", 67
Wickham's Fancy, 9, 50
Wickham, Pink, 50
Willow fly, 33
Wind, fishing with the, 3, 5
 "sufficient", 3, 67
 "whistling", 3, 67
Windy days, 4, 5
Wing cases or covers, 9, 10, 21, 76, 100, 102, 103, 105
Winged flies in the 'seventies, 4
 under water, 54, 56
Winging split-winged floaters (H. S. Hall), 4
Wire, gold, 100-101
 silver, 100-101
Wool, translucent, 98
Woolley, Roger, 11, 123
Wriggle of nymph, 22, 23, 73
Wye River, Derbyshire, 54

Yore River, 53
Yorkshire fisherman (Mr Reffitt) on Upper Test, 69

MINOR TACTICS OF
THE CHALK STREAM

Dedicated

TO MY FRIEND THE DRY-FLY PURIST, AND TO MY ENEMIES, IF I HAVE ANY

CONTENTS

	PAGE
NOTE TO THE SECOND EDITION	145
FOREWORD	147

CHAPTER

I. OF THE BEGINNING OF THINGS - - - 149
    OF THE INQUIRING MIND

II. SUBAQUEOUS HAPPENINGS IN NATURE - - - 154
    OF THE DROWNING OF DUNS AND OTHER
      INSECTS
    OF THE STAGES IN A RISE OF DUNS

III. SUBAQUEOUS HAPPENINGS IN ART - - - 158
    OF MEDICINE FOR BULGERS
    OF UNDER-WATER TAKING, ITS INDICATIONS,
      AND THE TIME TO STRIKE
    OF ROUGH WATER AND GREY-BROWN SHADOW

IV. SUPPLEMENTARY IN THE MATTER OF FLIES - - 165
    OF WET-FLY DRESSINGS FOR CHALK STREAMS
    OF THE IMPORTANCE OF COLOUR OF TYING SILK
    OF THE IMITATION OF NYMPHS, ETC.

V. SPECIAL CONDITIONS AND WET-FLY SOLUTIONS - - 174
    NERVES
    OF THE TROUT OF GLASSY GLIDES
    OF THE WET FLY IN POOLS, BAYS, AND EDDIES
    OF THE JUDICIOUS USE OF THE MOON
    OF THE WET-FLY OIL TIP
    OF GENERALSHIP AND THE WET FLY
    A POTTED TROUT, AND ONE OTHER
    OF TWO SATURDAY AFTERNOONS

VI. UNCLASSIFIED - - - - - - 189
    OF HOVERING
    OF THE PORPOISE ROLL

CHAPTER	PAGE
VII. SUNDRY CONSIDERATIONS	192
OF THE RELATION OF PATTERN TO POSITION	
OF THE USE OF SPINNERS	
OF GENERAL FEEDERS	
ON ATTENTION TO CASUAL FEEDERS	
OF THE FREQUENTATION OF DITCHES	
OF THE NEGOTIATION OF TAILERS	
OF THE FASCINATION OF BRIDGES	
VIII. MAINLY TACTICAL	207
OF THE DELIBERATE DRAG	
IN THE GLASS EDGE	
OF THE CROSS-COUNTRY CAST	
WHAT TUSSOCKS ARE FOR	
OF THE ALLEGED MARCH BROWN	
OF GENERAL FLIES	
IX. CONSIDERATIONS MORAL, TACTICAL, PSYCHOLOGICAL, AND INCIDENTAL	217
OF FAITH	
OF THE BANK OF VANTAGE	
OF COURAGE AND THE JEOPARDIZING OF TUPPENCE HA'PENNY	
OF IMPOSSIBLE PLACES	
OF THE USE OF THE LANDING-NET	
OF THE WEEDING TROUT	
OF THE LIGHT ROD ON CHALK STREAMS	
AND OF WET-FLY CASTING	
X. FRANKLY IRRELEVANT	236
A DRY FLY MEMORY	
XI. ETHICS OF THE WET FLY	239
XII. APOLOGIA	243

NOTE TO THE SECOND EDITION

It would ill become me if I allowed a Second Edition of "Minor Tactics of the Chalk Stream" to go to the public without expressing to those writers who have dealt with my volume in the Press my grateful sense of the generosity with which, whether they were or were not in agreement with the main object of the work —the endeavour to put the wet fly in what I conceive to be its right place on the chalk stream—they have one and all received it. In the fifty or so Press notices, short and long, I find, without exception, an absence of the harsh word, and a pervading urbane and kindly spirit which is of the true Waltonian still. Such fault as has been found has in the main been that I have shown undue timidity in dealing with the pretensions of the dry-fly purist. To that criticism I should like to reply that in dedicating my book to my *friend* the dry-fly purist I was using no idle word—that in asking him to make room for the wet fly beside the dry fly as a branch of the art of chalk-stream angling, I knew myself to be making a claim on him which he would not willingly concede, and I was determined that no harsh or provocative word of mine should give offence to any of the many good friends, good anglers, and good fellows who would not—at the first onset, at any rate—find themselves able to see eye to eye with me.

I take leave to hope that the interval since the first publication of "Minor Tactics" has brought a good few of them round to the view that, without ousting the dry fly from pride of place as major tactics of the chalk stream, the wet fly has its subsidiary, but still important, place of honour in chalk-stream fishing.

FOREWORD

RISING from the perusal of "Dry-Fly Fishing in Theory and Practice," on its publication by Mr. F. M. Halford in 1889, I think I was at one with most anglers of the day in feeling that the last word had been written on the art of chalk-stream fishing —so sane, so clear, so comprehensive, is it, so just and so in accord with one's own experience. Twenty years have gone by since then without my having had either occasion or inclination to go back at all upon this view of that, the greatest work, in my opinion, which has ever seen the light on the subject of angling for trout and grayling; and it is still, as regards that side of the subject with which it deals, all that I then believed it. But one result of the triumph of the dry fly, of which that work was the crown and consummation, was the obliteration from the minds of men, in much less than a generation, of all the wet-fly lore which had served many generations of chalk-stream anglers well. The effect was stunning, hypnotic, submerging; and in these days, if one excepts a few eccentrics who have been nurtured on the wet fly on other waters, and have little experience of chalk streams, one would find few with any notion that anything but the dry fly could be effectively used upon Hampshire rivers, or that the wet fly was ever used there. I was for years myself under the spell; and it is the purpose of the ensuing pages to tell, for the benefit of the angling community, by what processes, by what stages, I have been led into a sustained effort to recover for this generation, and to transmute into forms suited to the modern conditions of sport on the chalk stream, the old wet-fly art, to be used as a supplement to, and in no sense to supplant or rival, the beautiful art of which Mr. F. M. Halford is the prophet. How far my effort has been successful I must leave my readers to judge. I myself feel that in making it I have widened my angling horizon, and that I have added enormously to the interest and charm of my angling days as well as to my chances of success, and that, too, by the use of no methods which the most rigid purist could rightly condemn, but by a difficult, delicate, fascinating, and entirely legitimate form of the art, well worthy of the naturalist sportsman.

In the course of my too rare excursions to the river-side, I have elaborated some devices, methods of attack and handling, which I have found of service, some applicable to wet-fly, some to dry-fly fishing, some to both. In the hope that these may be of interest or service, I have included papers upon them.

In conclusion I should like to express my gratitude to the proprietors of the *Field*, for permission to reprint a number of papers contributed by me to that journal over the signature "Seaforth and Soforth," which come within the scope of the work; and to Mr. H. T. Sheringham, for his invaluable advice and assistance in the arrangement of these papers.

December, 1909.   G.E.M. SKUES.

CHAPTER I

OF THE BEGINNING OF THINGS

OF THE INQUIRING MIND.

I READ recently in that fine novel, "A Superfluous Woman," a sentence enunciating a principle of wide application, to which anglers might with advantage give heed : "We ought not so much to name mistakes disaster as the common practice of servile imitation and faint-hearted acquiescence." In no art are its practitioners more slavishly content "jurare in verba magistri" than in angling. Tradition and authority are so much, and individual observation and experiment so little.

There is, indeed, this excuse for the novice, that, going back to the authorities of the past after much experiment, he will find that they know in substance all, or practically all, that, apart from the advance of mechanical conveniences and entomological science, is known in the present day. The difficulty is to dissociate the dead knowledge, which is reading or imitation, from the live knowledge, which is experience. And if these pages have any purpose more than another, it is not to lay down the law or to dogmatize, but to urge brother anglers to keep an open and observant mind, to experiment, and to bring to their angling, not book knowledge, but the result of their own observation, trials, and experiments—failures as well as successes.

In all humility is this written, for I look back upon many years when it was my sole ambition to follow in the steps of the masters of chalk-stream angling, and to do what was laid down for me—that, and no other; and I look back with some shame at the slowness to take a hint from experience which has marked my angling career. It was in the year 1892, after some patient years of dry-fly practice, that I had my first experience of the efficacy of the wet fly on the Itchen. It was a September day, at once blazing and muggy. Black gnats were thick upon the water, and from 9.30 a.m. or so the trout were smutting freely.

In those days, with "Dry-Fly Fishing in Theory and Practice" at my fingers' ends, I began with the prescription, "Pink Wickham on 00 hook," followed it with "Silver Sedge on 00 hook, Red Quill on 00 hook, orange bumble, and furnace." I also tried two or three varieties of smut, and I rang the changes more than once. My gut was gossamer, and, honestly, I don't think I made more mistakes than usual; but three o'clock arrived, and my creel was still "clean," when I came to a bend from which ran, through a hatch, a small current of water which fed a carrier. Against the grating which protected the hatch-hole was generally a large pile of weed, and to-day was no exception. Against it lay collected a film of scum, alive with black gnats, and among them I saw a single dark olive dun lying spent. I had seen no others of his kind during the day, but I knotted on a Dark Olive Quill on a single cipher hook, and laid siege to a trout which was smutting steadily in the next little bay. The fly was a shop-tied one, beautiful to look at when new, but as a floater it was no success. The hackle was a hen's, and the dye only accentuated its natural inclination to sop up water. The oil tip had not yet arrived, and so it came about that, after the wetting it got in the first recovery, it no sooner lit on the water on the second cast than it went under. A moment later I became aware of a sort of crinkling little swirl in the water, ascending from the place where I conceived my fly might be. I was somewhat too quick in putting matters to the proof, and when my line came back to me there was no fly. I mounted another, and assailed the next fish, and to my delight exactly the same thing occurred, except that this time I did not strike too hard.

OF THE BEGINNING OF THINGS

The trout's belly contained a solid ball of black gnats, and not a dun of any sort. The same was the case with all the four brace more which I secured in the next hour or so by precisely the same methods. Yet each took the Dark Olive at once when offered under water, while all day the trout had been steadily refusing the recognized floating lures recommended by the highest authority. It was a lesson which ought to have set me thinking and experimenting, but it didn't. I put by the experience for use on the next September smutting day, and I have never had quite such another, so close, so sweltering, with such store of smuts, and the trout taking them so steadily and so freely.

It was a September day two or three years later when I had another hint as pointed and definite as one could get from the hind-leg of a mule, but I didn't take it. There was a cross-stream wind from the west, with a favour of north in it, and all the duns—and there were droves of them—drifted in little fleets close hugging the east bank, where the trout were lined up in force to deal with them, and feeding steadily. Fishing from the west bank, I stuck to four fish which I satisfied myself were good ones, and in over two hours' fishing I never put them down. I tried over them all my repertoire. I battered them with Dark Olive Quill, Medium Olive Quill, Gold-ribbed Hare's Ear, Red Quill (two varieties), Grey Quill and Blue Quill, Ogden's Fancy, and Wickham, and at the end I left them rising with undiminished energy, and went and sat down and had my lunch. Then I sought another fish, and began again, when suddenly it occurred to me that I had not tried the old-fashioned moles-fur-bodied, snipe-winged Blue Dun. I had only a solitary specimen, and that was tied with a hen's hackle; but such as it was, and greatly distrusting its floating powers, I tied it on. I did not err in my distrust, for after a cast or two it was hopelessly waterlogged. I dried it as well as I could in my handkerchief, and despatched it once more on its mission. It went under almost as it lit, just above a capital trout, but for all that it was taken immediately. The next trout, and the next, and the next, took it with equal promptitude; one was small, and had to go back, but the others were quite nice average fish.

Then, in my eagerness, I was too hard on my gossamer gut when the next trout took my fly, and he kept it. I had no more of these Blue Duns, and I did not get another fish till the evening.

Still I did not realize that I was on the edge of an adventure, nor yet did I realize whither I was tending when Mr. F. M. Halford told me how a well-known Yorkshire angler had been fishing with him on the Test, and, by means of a wet fly admirably fished without the slightest drag, had contrived to basket some trout on a difficult water.*

Indeed, it was several years later that, after fluking upon a successful experience of the wet fly on a German river which in general was a distinctively dry-fly stream, I began to speculate seriously upon the possibility of a systematic use of the wet fly in aid of the dry fly upon chalk streams. In conversation with the late Mr. Godwin (held in affectionate remembrance by many members of the Fly-fishers' Club, and, indeed, by all who knew him), who had seen the very beginnings of the dry fly on the Itchen, and remembered well and had practised the methods which preceded it, I learned how, fishing downstream with long and flexible rods (thirteen or fourteen feet long), and keeping the light hair reel-line off the water as much as possible, these early fathers of the craft had drifted their wet flies over the tails of weeds, where the trout lay in open gravel patches, and caught baskets of which the modern dry-fly man might well be proud.

I gathered, however, that a downstream ruffle of wind was a practical necessity; and as I could not pick my days, and such as I could take were few and far between, I realized that, even if they appealed to me—which they did not—these methods would not do for me, as I might, and often did, find the river glassy smooth, but that, if I were to succeed, it must be by a wet-fly

* See "An Angler's Autobiography," by F. M. Halford, p. 69 (1903).

modification of the dry-fly method of upstream casting to individual fish.

I could not believe that the habits of the trout were so changed as to make this impossible, and I began to look for opportunities to experiment. The bulging trout presented the most obvious case, yet it was rather by a chain of circumstance than by the straightforward reasoning which now seems so simple and obvious that I was led into experiments along this line.

How I effected some sort of solution of the problem with a variant of Greenwell's Glory, and later on with Tup's Indispensable, is detailed elsewhere, as also are my experiments with the trout of glassy glides (who seldom break the surface to take a winged insect, presumably because of the drag), together with other fumblings in the search of truth; but from that time forth I have seldom neglected an opportunity to test the wet fly on chalk-stream trout. It may be that on many occasions I have used the wet fly when the dry would have been more lucrative. On the other hand, I have found it furnish me with sport on occasions when and in places where the dry fly offered no encouragement, nor any prospect of aught but casual and fluky success, and I have provided myself with a method which forms an admirable supplement to the dry fly, and has frequently given me a good basket in apparently hopeless conditions, and in the smoothest of water and the brightest of weather.

CHAPTER II

SUBAQUEOUS HAPPENINGS IN NATURE

OF THE DROWNING OF DUNS AND OTHER INSECTS.

It has been advanced as an argument against the use of the wet fly, that duns and the other small insects which drift down upon the surface of a stream are never seen by the fish under water, and that a wet fly is therefore an unnatural object, especially if winged. "Never" is a big word, and I venture to think the case is overstated. I have watched an eddy with little swirling whirlpools in it for an hour together, and again and again I have seen little groups of flies caught in one or other of the whirls, sucked under and thrown scatterwise through the water, to drift some distance before again reaching the surface.

Anyone who has kept water-insects in spirit for observation or mounting is aware that they readily become water-logged, and by no means insist on floating. Again, we have it on the best authority that certain of the spinners descend to the river-bed to lay their eggs,* and probably, that function performed, they ascend again through the water, giving the trout a chance while in transit. Thus the trout may well be familiar with winged insects under water. Even if he were not, it may be doubted whether he is sufficiently intelligent to reject a thing which he fancies he has found good to eat on the surface merely because it happens to be below. Indeed, experience so conclusively proves that trout will take the winged fly under water that those who repudiate both these propositions are upon the horns of a dilemma. Many

* See "Dry-Fly Entomology," p. 32 (1897).

hackled flies are more or less—and generally less—careful imitations of nymphs or larvæ. But of these more anon.

OF THE STAGES IN A RISE OF DUNS.

It has often been the subject of admiring comment that, before ever the angler can see a single fly in air or upon water, the trout will have lined up under the banks, and settled at the tails of weed-beds, and have begun to take toll of insect life; and many have commented on the startling unanimity with which trout begin to feed all at once all over a river or length. Some seem to suppose that, with a quick appreciation of values of temperature, atmosphere, barometric pressure, and what not, the trout discern when the flies will rise, and are there in readiness. Is it necessary to suppose anything so far-fetched? It has often seemed to me that swifts, swallows, and martins can and do detect in advance the preparations for a rise in the swarming of nymphs released from weed or gravel, or whatever their particular fastness may be, and borne down the current. This precedes the actual hatch for a period greater or less according to temperature, pressure, and perhaps other little-understood conditions; and so it happens that no trout that is not "by ordinar'" stupid could fail to appreciate that game is afoot, and to put himself in position to enjoy the sport.

If one goes down to the bottom of the High in Winchester, near by King Alfred's statue, and peers between the railings, one may generally see several brace of handsome trout; and if one takes some new bread and presses it together in little balls hard enough to make it sink, but not sink too fast, and throws it to the trout, one may see some most beautiful catching, neater than that of the most finished fielder in the slips. So when the nigh-upon-hatching nymphs are being hurried down, your trout shall enjoy some pretty fielding before the bulk of the quarry come near enough to the surface to attract attention to the trout's movements by any swirl or break on the surface. If the trout be lying out on the weeds from which the nymphs are issuing, you shall see the trout swashing about in the shallow water covering the weed-beds, in pursuit of the nymphs, and presenting the phenomenon known as "bulging." This is the first stage of the rise.

Presently, as the swarm of drifting nymphs becomes more numerous, escaping units, first in sparse, then in increasing numbers, reach the surface, burst their swathing envelopes, and spread their canvas to the gales as *subimagines*. Presently the trout find attention to the winged fly more advantageous—as presenting more food, or food obtained with less exertion than the nymphs —and turn themselves to it in earnest. This is the second stage. Often it is much deferred. Conditions of which we know nothing keep back the hatch, perhaps send many of the nymphs back to cover to await a more favourable opportunity another day; so it occasionally happens that, while the river seems mad with bulging fish, the hatch of fly that follows or partly coincides with this orgy is insignificant. But, good, bad, or indifferent, it measures the extent of the dry-fly purist's opportunity.

Good, bad, or indifferent, it presently peters out, and at times with startling suddenness all the life and movement imparted to the surface by the rings of rising fish are gone, and it would be easy for one who knew not the river to say: "There are no trout in it." For all that, there are pretty sure to be left a sprinkling, often more than a sprinkling, of unsatisfied fish which are willing to feed, and can be caught if the angler knows how; and these will hang about for a while until they, too, give up in despair and go home, or seek consolation in tailing. Often these will take a dry fly, but an imitation of a nymph or a broken or submerged fly is a far stronger temptation. This is the third stage.

Now, the dry-fly purist is quite entitled to his own opinions, and to restrict himself to the second stage; but if there be other anglers who are willing to vary their methods, who can and do catch their trout, not only in the second stage, but also in the first and the third, and if their methods spoil no sport for others, who shall say that they are wrong in availing themselves of all three stages of a rise of duns?

I remember well one day late in May when the three stages were excellently well marked. There was a bright sun, a light breeze from the east with a touch of south in it, and I was on the water about 9.30, and took the left bank, with the wind behind my hand. No fish were rising, but on reaching the waterside I almost stumbled on top of a trout which stood poised over a clear gravel patch under my own bank. Fortunately, however, I withdrew without his seeing or suspecting me. My pale-dressed Greenwell's Glory trailed in the water, and I delivered it without flick, well wet, a foot or so above the spot where I had marked my fish. There was no break of the surface, but a sort of smooth shallow hump of the water about the size of a dinner-plate, with a dip in the middle, as the fish turned and I pulled into him. Presently I saw a brace bulging vigorously over some bright green weeds. It was not the first or the tenth time that my sunken Greenwell covered the fish that one of them came; but when he did there was no doubt about it, and he joined number one in the basket. Two more followed in a short time, unable to resist the same lure. Then it seemed to fail of its effect, though the river was freely dotted with rings, and after wasting much time I tumbled to the situation, and changed to a floating No. 1 Whitchurch—most effective of Yellow Duns—on a cipher hook. The effect was immediate, but I had put it off too long, and when I looked up from basketing my third trout to the Whitchurch the rise had worn out. But I was not done yet. I changed to a Tup's Indispensable dressed to sink, and, fishing upstream wet in likely runs and places, I made up my five brace before I knocked off for lunch.

CHAPTER III

SUBAQUEOUS HAPPENINGS IN ART

OF MEDICINE FOR BULGERS.

FOR many a year bulging trout were the despair of my life, and in those days I would gladly have said "Amen" to the opinion expressed in a letter to the *Fishing Gazette* of March 13, 1909, by the angler who writes over the pen-name of "Ballygunge," that when trout were bulging you "might as well chuck your hat at them" as a fly. Many times had I vainly plied them with Gold-ribbed Hare's Ear, as recommended by Mr. F. M. Halford, as well as most of the current imitations of duns on the water, and Wickhams, Tags, and other fancy flies to boot. Hoping against hope, I never gave up trying for those aggravating fish, and one day, towards the end of a bad exhibition of bulging by the trout, I actually caught a brace, and lost a third, on a Pope's Green Nondescript*—a dun tied with starling wing, red hackle and whisk, and a dark green body ribbed with broad flat gold.

On many occasions since I have found that fly kill well at the beginning of a rise, and it may be that on the occasion spoken of the trout which I got were on the verge of giving up bulging in favour of the winged dun. But I was not satisfied. Then the recollection of a visit to the Tweed struck me with the notion that on that water all the trout practically bulged all the time, and that with their wet-fly patterns Tweed anglers were able to give a good account of themselves, and I searched among

* This pattern is also very attractive to tailers. See "The Way of a Trout with a Fly," p. 118.

Tweed patterns for the nearest analogue to Pope's Green Nondescript. I thought I found it in Greenwell's Glory, if varied by exchanging for the hen blackbird wing a starling wing. The likeness was not very exact, but it was close enough to experiment on. The point that I wanted to achieve was to combine with the colours of Pope's Green Nondescript the type of dressing special to the Tweed Greenwell's Glory. Rough, slim upright wings, well split, and standing well apart when wet, made of several thicknesses of feather so as to absorb water, and not to give it up readily when cast; body spare, consisting of the waxed primrose tying silk only, closely ribbed with fine gold wire, and one or at most two turns of a furnace hen's hackle with ginger points, no whisk (whisks only help flotation), and a rather rank hook to take the fly under. The type of dressing is to be found applied to all his patterns in Webster's "Angler and the Loop Rod."

Whether it was because I had faith in my medicine, or whether any other cause was at work, I know not, but the experiment was, despite some misses due to failure to judge the right moment to pull home the hook, an immediate success.

Bulging trout are bold feeders, and seem to mind being cast over less than do those which are taking surface food; but they are much more difficult to cover accurately, because they rush from side to side and up and down, and the odds are that, if you cast to one spot, the trout is careering off in pursuit of a nymph to right or left of it. But once the trout sees the fly, the chances of his taking it are far better than are the chances that a surface-feeding trout will take the floating dun which covers him. The fly is allowed to drag in the stream, so as to be thoroughly wet, and is then cast upstream to the feeding fish in all respects like a floating fly, except that it is not dried or allowed to float. The weight of the reel-line will probably be enough to dry the gut, so that the risk of lining your trout is minimized, only the fly and the first link or so of gut going under before it reaches him. I found it best to tie this pattern on gut, and, dressed as described, it has been worth many a good bulger to me, apart from its value for general purposes.

Later on the value of Tup's Indispensable fished wet impressed me much, and its resemblance to a nymph induced me to give it a trial upon bulging trout. For wet-fly purposes this is as near the dressing as I am at liberty to give: Primrose tying silk lapped down the hook from head to tail, a pale blue or creamy whisk of hen's feather as soft as possible and not long, three or four turns of coarser untwisted primrose sewing silk at the tail, body rather fat, of a mixed dubbing of a creamy pink (invented by Mr. R. S. Austin, the well-known angler and fly-dresser of Tiverton),* and a soft blue dun hackle, very short in the fibre, at the head, the dressing being preferably finished at the shoulder behind the hackle. When this fly is thoroughly soaked it has a wonderfully soft and translucent, insect-like effect. It proved even more successful than Greenwell's Glory, and with one or other I am almost always able to give a good account of bulgers instead of coming empty away.

OF UNDER-WATER TAKING, ITS INDICATIONS, AND THE TIME TO STRIKE.

Friends with whom I have discussed the use of the upstream wet fly on chalk streams have frequently said to me: "But how are you to know when the trout takes, and when to strike?" It is a very pertinent question, and the answer is not to be given in a word. Often the indications which bid you pull home the hook are so subtle and inconspicuous that the angler is at a loss to account for the miracle which is evidenced by his hooped rod and protesting reel; but even in the roughest water something helps the angler to divine the moment for action. In a subsequent section, under the heading "The Grey-Brown Shadow," will be found an account of a day's sport with the wet fly in an up-

* Now, alas! some years deceased.

stream wind so rough as to throw the river into waves. The flash of the fish as it turns to take the fly may often be seen, so dimly and so momentarily as to be apt to escape notice if one does not know what to look for; but I have on several occasions even divined it through water which reflected a bright white glare, and seemed opaque to the eye. If on these occasions a hooked trout had not proved the truth of my observation, I could not have sworn to having certainly seen anything move; but there through the surface, which looked at the angle of view impenetrable to the eye, I did seem to glimpse a faint pink flash that corresponded to no movement on the surface, and there was the fish soundly hooked, and no fluke about it.

Often under an opposite bank, when the light will not permit you to see your gut or fly, you will see a trout suddenly ascending to near the top of the water, and as suddenly sinking; then, if you tighten, ten to one your hook is firmly in his jaws, and you see him shaking his head savagely at the unexpected restraint upon his liberty ere he makes his first rush.

When fish are bulging, the moment of taking the fly is generally marked by a swirl, and the angler should strike immediately. Fortunately, a wet-fly strike, even if misconceived or mistimed, is far less likely, so long as the fish is clean missed and not lined, to alarm him than is a strike with the dry fly, because the wet fly comes out through the water at a point far below the fish instead of being drawn along the surface.

In glassy glides, which are always fast water, one either sees the fish turn to the fly, or, if the light prevents it, one sees a little crinkle, or break, work up through the water to the surface, which warns the angler to strike. Often the gut lying on the surface goes under as the fish draws in the fly, and alike in daylight and moonlight it acts as a float; and even if the fly be taken too deep below water for any other indication to be in time, it will warn the angler to attend to business. An ingenious angler, as elsewhere explained, has conceived and utilized successfully the idea of oiling his gut cast for fishing wet directly upstream in rapid water, and an excellent device it is for its occasion.

But perhaps the commonest indication of an under-water taking in water of slow or moderate pace is an almost imperceptible shallow humping of the water over the trout. It is caused by the turn of the fish as he takes the fly, and when the angler sees it it is time to fasten. If he waits until the swirl has reached and broken the surface (and it may not be violent enough to do so), he may be too late. If the fly drops directly over the fish, that shallow hump seems often almost simultaneous with the lighting of the fly; but if the cast be wide, your trout will not infrequently dart a yard or more to a wet fly—when for a dry fly he would do no such thing—and then the angler has a warning of the coming of the shallow hump on the surface which tells him that the iron is hot. It may be questioned, however, whether it is not more difficult to time correctly the strike for which one has had such warning than one which comes without warning.

In my experience, the trout which takes under-water is generally very soundly hooked. A trout taking floaters on the surface frequently sips them in through a narrowly-opened slit of mouth, but an under-water feeder draws in the fly by an extension of the gills which carries it in with a full gulp of water.

In the effort to divine the indications which call for striking with the wet fly I confess I find a subtle fascination and charm, and, when success attends me, a satisfaction beside which the successful hooking of a fish which rises to my floating fly seems second-rate in its sameness and comparative obviousness and monotony of achievement.

OF ROUGH WATER AND GREY-BROWN SHADOW.

It was blowing up freshly from the south-west as the train ran into Winchester one April a year or two back, and ere the water-meadows were reached the distinct bite in the wind had given ample warning that, maugre the crisp yellow sunshine, 11.30 clanging from the cathedral spires left ample time to get down to the water-side and put rod and tackle together before the big dark olives or the smaller and rather lighter olives, which warn one to put up a Gold-ribbed Hare's Ear, put in an appearance. April was three parts through, yet the backwardness of the season made conditions correspond more nearly to three weeks earlier in the normal year.

Soon everything was in readiness, and a couple of dark **Rough Olives**, tied on gut, with dark starling wing, heron herl body dyed in onion dye and ribbed with fine gold wire, and hackle and whisk of ginger, lightly dyed olive, were put into the damper to soak, on the chance that the wet fly might pay better than the dry.

Noon and the quarter-past chimed from the belfry, and then a big dark olive drifted on to an eddy near by, and, lifted out on the meshes of a landing-net, was identified. The hint was enough. One of the flies in soak—tied on No. 1 hooks—was knotted on, and the surface was scanned for the first dimple. Presently it was located—such a tiny, infinitesimal, dacelike dimple, hinting rather than proving the movement of a trout. It was hardly noticeable in the turmoil made by the strong ruffle of the upstream wind against the somewhat full current of the stream. It was rather far across for accurate casting in such a wind, and presently a sudden gust slammed the line down upon the spot with such a splash as no self-respecting trout could be expected to endure.

A movement upstream was prescribed by the conditions, and presently another dimple like the last was spotted in a more favourable position. It was repeated after an interval, but no fly was to be seen on the surface; so, without an attempt at drying, the Rough Olive was despatched on his mission, and lit a foot or so above the spot. Again, and once more, it did so, and then there was a hint of a grey-brown flicker in the hollow of a wave. By instinct rather than reason the hand went up, and the arch of the rod showed that the steel had gone home. In due course the trout—a fish of fourteen inches—was landed, and the angler proceeded upward.

He soon found, however, that to reach and cover the trout satisfactorily it behoved him to cross, and tackle them from the other side, and he made his way to the footbridge. On the way down, on the main stream he saw another hint of a rise in midstream, where the waves were highest. The wind served him well, and the fly was over the trout in no time. For four or five casts there was no response; then again that grey-brown shadow for a moment in the trough of a wave, mounting rod, a screaming reel, and a vigorous trout was battling for his life.

Arrived presently at the desired spot, the wet Rough Olive was taken off and a dry-fly pattern mounted and duly oiled, and offered to three fish in succession, with the result that they all went down. Then back once more to the wet-fly, and thrice more ere 1.30 struck there was the faint flash of grey-brown under water, the same instinctive response, a spirited battle for life (successful in one instance), and then the rise petered out and not a fish was stirring. And though at 2.30 a strong rise of the smaller olive came on, and lasted till 4.30, keeping hundreds of swallows and martins busy, yet not another fish put up a neb. Perhaps it was because the sun had gone in.

There are those who wax indignant at the use of the wet fly on dry-fly waters. Yet it has a special fascination. The indications which tell your dry-fly angler when to strike are clear and unmistakable, but those which bid a wet-fly man raise his rod-point and draw in the steel are frequently so subtle, so evanescent and impalpable to the senses, that, when the bending rod assures him that he has divined aright, he feels an ecstasy as though he had performed a miracle each time.

CHAPTER IV

SUPPLEMENTARY IN THE MATTER OF FLIES

OF WET-FLY DRESSINGS FOR CHALK STREAMS.

ASSUMING that we have made up our minds to test the wet fly upon chalk streams, it must be taken as an axiom that the ordinary patterns of the dry fly will not do. They are built to dry and to float. The patterns required must be built to soak and to sink. Therefore bodies and hackles which throw the water must be rejected in favour of bodies and hackles which take up the water or readily enter it. So dubbed bodies in place of quills, hen hackles in place of cock's, and of these a minimum of turns in place of a maximum; and if whisks are used, they, too, must be soft and soppy. For the same reason, wing material, if employed, should be so arranged as to take up the maximum of water, and to let it go as unwillingly as possible. Furthermore, the bulk of material in proportion to the hook metal must be reduced as far as possible.

Given these requirements, let us look around, as I did, among all the various systems of wet-fly dressing in use, from John o' Groat's to Land's End, and see what features we ought to borrow from them. If we make up our minds, as I think we shall, that it is desirable to expose the body of our fly freely, we shall not adopt any system which lays the wings low over the back of the fly, that type being designed to secure what is called "a good entry" for a dragging fly, and we have nothing to do with dragging flies or any form of river raking or dredging, or with any flies which, like the Devonshire types, carry superabundance of bright cock's hackles. So we are limited to the systems which dress their flies with upright wings, like the Tweed and Clyde types, and to the soft hackled Yorkshire style.

The conditions, however, of our waters confine us to tiny patterns—Nos. 0 and 00 hooks in the vast majority of cases, and occasionally No. 1—and the supply of tiny soft absorbent hackles from birds other than poultry, sufficiently small to leave the body well exposed, is hardly to be had. So, taking one consideration with another, it would seem that the Tweed and Clyde patterns, being used on a broad and in many places equably-flowing river, will have advantages enough to invite a trial.

Now, what are the features of the Tweed and Clyde patterns? First there is the spare body, dressed with tying silk only, with or without wire ribbing, or lightly dubbed with soft fur, making an absorbent dubbing; then a small and lightly dressed soft hackle, two turns at the outside, close up behind a pair of wings tied in a bunch, and either left single or, preferably for our purposes, split in equal portions, and divided with the figure-of-eight application of the tying silk behind the wings and in front of the head, the whole tied on a rank, and not too light, round-bend hook.

It will be suggested that the trout does not see the winged dun under water. That is approximately, though not quite absolutely, true; but for all that, being in some respects rather a stupid person, he will not make much bones of the position of the fly with reference to the surface being incorrect if size and colour be right. It might be supposed, again, that a hackled pattern would better suggest the nymph stage than would a winged pattern. This may be true, but the theory has yet to be worked out in much detail before one can dogmatize about it. Elsewhere my preliminary efforts in this direction are described. Here I could say that the wings built up of a length of feather rolled into a bunch have the advantage of taking up a lot of water, and not releasing it readily; and they also assist to let the fly down more lightly on the water than so lightly dressed a fly would

SUPPLEMENTARY IN THE MATTER OF FLIES

fall but for the wings. To let a hackled fly down as lightly, one would need a lighter wire and a large hackle. The wings also help the fly to swim correctly in the water, with the weight of the straight, unsnecked, round-bend hook as the counterpoise to the parachute action of the wings.

My own belief is that wet flies tied on gut swim better and hook better than those tied on eyed hooks. As the drying action of casting is reduced to a minimum, they are not so ready to go at the neck as when used as dry flies; but if the angler prefers it, there is no reason why he should not use eyed hooks, though snecked bends of any kind and upturned eyes are deprecated. Down-eyed hooks, round, unsnecked square-bend, and Limerick, in the order named, are recommended.

When immediate sinking in rather fast water is required, additional weight can be got by tying on a second hook, and making the fly what is technically known as a "double." These are more easily tied on gut than on eyed hooks, though there is a maker who supplies eyed hooks for doubles in sizes Nos. 1, 0, and 00, one packet containing the eyed hook, and the other the shorter-shanked companion hook to be lashed on. In either case the hooks have to be separated with the thumb-nail, so as to stand at an angle of 45 to 60 degrees before using. Lest it should be suggested that these double hooks, fished wet, lend themselves to a form of snatching, let me say that I can only recall a single instance of a trout being hooked on a wet double otherwise than fairly in the mouth, and in the course of my experiments I have given them an extensive trial.

The range of wet-fly patterns required is not extensive. I have found the following serve all practical purposes:

1. ROUGH OLIVE.
    Wings: Darkest starling.
    Body: Heron herl from wing feather dyed brown-olive, and ribbed with fine gold wire.
    Legs: Dirty brown-olive hen hackle, with dark centre and yellowish-brown points.
    Hook: No. 1.

2. GREENWELL'S GLORY
   Wings: Hen blackbird, dark starling, medium starling, or light starling (lighter as season advances).
   Body: Primrose or yellow tying silk, more or less waxed (lighter as season advances), ribbed with fine gold wire
   Legs: Dark furnace hen hackle (black centre, with cinnamon points) to medium honey dun (lighter as season advances).
   Hook: No. 1, 0, or 00.

3. BLUE DUN.
   Wings: Snipe.
   Body: Water-rat on primrose or yellow tying silk. Vary body by dressing with undyed heron's herl from the wing, and ribbing with fine gold or silver wire.
   Legs: Medium blue hen.
   Hook: No. 1 or 0.

4. IRON BLUE.*
   Wings: Tomtit's tail.
   Body: Mole's fur on claret tying silk.
   Legs: Honey-dun hen with red points.
   Hook: No. 0 or 00.

5. WATERY DUN.
   Wings: Palest starling.
   Body: Hare's poll or buff opossum on primrose tying silk.
   Legs: Ginger hen's hackle.
   Hook: No. 00.

6. HARE'S EAR.
   Wings: Dark or Medium starling.
   Body: Hare's fur from lobe at root of ear; rib, narrowest gold tinsel or fine gold wire.
   Legs: A few fibres picked out or placed between the strands of the silk and spun.
   Hook: No. 1 or 0.

7. BLACK GNAT.
   Wings: Palest snipe rolled and reversed.
   Body: Black tying silk with two turns of black ostrich herl or knob of black silk at shoulder.
   Legs: Black hen or cock starling's crest, two turns at most.
   Hook: No. 00.

It will be observed that hooks a size larger than those employed for floaters can often be used. Nymphs *are* slightly larger than their duns.

The very short range of hackled patterns is dealt with later.

* But see "The Way of a Trout with a Fly," p. 108, for a much better hackled pattern.

SUPPLEMENTARY IN THE MATTER OF FLIES

OF THE IMPORTANCE OF THE COLOUR OF TYING SILK IN DUBBED FLIES.

Years ago I spent a week upon the Teme, fishing wet, and I remember looking down one sunny morning upon my cast in shallow water, and being struck by the appearance of my Yellow Dun. The body was dubbed with primrose wool, but though, while dry or in the air, every turn of the tying silk was completely hidden, yet, looking down upon the fly in the water, I could see every turn distinctly, and the dubbing was scarcely noticeable, and I was glad that the tying silk harmonized so perfectly with the hue of the dubbing.

The importance of the base colour of the tying silk was still more strongly brought home to me a day or two later. I had tied some imitations of a pale watery dun which was on the water with a pale starling wing, light ginger hackle and whisk, and a mixture of opossum and hare's poll for dubbing; but some I had tied with pale orange silk, and some with that rich maroon colour called Red Ant in Mr. Aldam's series of silks. The grayling took those tied with pale orange freely, but would not look at those tied with Red Ant.

It may be of less consequence for floating flies, but for wet flies I have since always been careful to have the tying silk either harmonious with the colour of the natural subimago, or corresponding to the colour of the spinner. For instance, for an Iron Blue Dun I should use claret silk dubbed with mole's fur or water-rat; for the old-fashioned mole's fur Blue Dun, primrose to heighten the olive effect in the dark blue; primrose silk also for a Hare's Ear; in the Willow-Fly, orange silk under the mole's fur or water-rat; in the Grannom, green very darkly waxed, or black; and so on. The fact is that the transparency of fur and feather is marvellous. A starling's wing looks much denser than a dun's, but place it over print, and you can read every word through; and fur is practically as transparent when wet.

OF THE IMITATION OF NYMPHS, CADDIS, ALDER LARVÆ, AND SHRIMPS.

For some time after my introduction to Tup's Indispensable I used it only as a dry fly, but one July I put it over a fish without avail, and cast it a second time without drying it. It was dressed with a soft hackle, and at once went under, and the trout turned at it and missed. Again I cast, and again the trout missed, to fasten soundly at the next offer. It was a discovery for me, and I tried the pattern wet over a number of fish on the same shallow, with most satisfactory results. I thus satisfied myself that Tup's Indispensable could be used as a wet fly; and, indeed, when soaked its colours merge and blend so beautifully that is is hardly singular; and it was a remarkable imitation of a nymph I got from a trout's mouth.

The next step was to try it on bulging fish, and to my great delight I found it even more attractive than Greenwell's Glory. It was the foundation of a small range of nymph patterns, but for under-water feeders, whether bulging of otherwise, I seldom need anything but Tup's Indispensable, dressed with a very short, soft henny hackle in place of the bright honey or rusty dun used for the floating pattern. The next I tried was a Blue-winged Olive. There was a hatch of this pernicious insect* one afternoon. The floating pattern is always a failure with me, and in anticipation I had tied some nymphs of appropriate colour of body, and hackled with a single turn of the tiniest blue hackle of the merlin. It enabled me to get two or three excellent trout which were taking blue-winged olive nymphs greedily under the opposite bank, and which, or rather the first of which, like their predecessors, had refused to respond to a floating imitation. The body was a mixture of medium olive seal's fur and bear's hair close to the skin, tied with primrose silk, the whisk being short and soft, from the spade-shaped feather found on the shoulder of a blue dun cock.

* But see the chapter on B.W.O., p. 176 of "The Way of a Trout with a Fly," for my maturer opinion of this insect.

SUPPLEMENTARY IN THE MATTER OF FLIES

Another pattern, successful in the last two months of the season, is dressed with a very short palish-blue dun or honey dun hen's hackle, a body of hare's poll tied on pale primrose silk, with or without a small gold tag and palest ginger whisks. But it is evident that on this subject I am only at the beginning of inquiry. Of course there is nothing very new in the idea of imitating nymphs. The half stone is just a nymph generally ruined by over-hackling.

In July, 1908, I caught an Itchen fish one afternoon, and on examining his mouth I found a dark olive nymph. My fly-dressing materials were with me, and I found I had a seal's fur which, with a small admixture of bear's hair, dark brown and woolly, from close to the skin, enabled me to reproduce exactly the colours of the natural insect. I dressed the imitation with short, soft, dark blue whisks, body of the mixed dubbing tied with well-waxed bright yellow silk, and bunched at the shoulder to suggest wing-cases, the lower part of the body being ribbed with fine gold wire. Two turns of a very short, dark rusty dun hackle completed the imitation, much to my satisfaction.

Apparently it was no less agreeable to the trout, for, beginning to fish next morning at ten o'clock, I found six fish rising on a shallow. I began with a small Red Sedge, as no dun was yet on the water, and missed several of them. Then, putting up Pope's Green Nondescript, I again missed three fish in succession. I then bethought myself of my nymph, and, knotting it on, in a few minutes I had five of the six fish, and had lost the other. I then found a trout feeding in a run, evidently under water. I made a miscast at him, and he came a yard across to take the nymph, but did not take a good hold, for I lost him, only to secure a better fish a few moments later. It then came on to blow and pelt with rain in such sort as to render it no sort of pleasure to continue fishing, and I knocked off at eleven o'clock, with three brace as the result of an hour's fishing.

I have made me a shallow spoon-shaped net of butterfly-net

material to attach to the ring of my landing-net. It has the advantage of taking anything which comes down the stream, whether on or under the surface, and its practical use demonstrates itself in more ways than one. For instance, in September, 1909, I went down to the river about 9.30, and, having put my rod together, sank my net in the water, and watched for what came down. There were a number of tiny diptera, but no trace of dun or nymph. I therefore concluded that it would be some time before the trout would be lined up under the banks, and that I could safely go away for an hour, and try certain carriers where the feeding of fish is not dependent on the rise. I did this, and put in over an hour's exciting, if not very remunerative, sport before returning to the main river. The rise came on about 11.30. But for my net I might have wasted all the time on the bank, instead of conducting a siege of three very handsome trout, and bringing up two of them.

On occasion I have found a Dotterel dun tied with yellow tying silk on a No. 00 hook, and hackled with the tiniest dotterel hackle, after the manner of Stewart (*i.e.*, not hackled all at the head, but palmer-wise for halfway down the short body), quite remunerative fished wet. This, I imagine, is taken for a dun emerging.

But it is not only duns whose nymphal stages may be imitated. I borrowed a tube containing some nearly full-grown larvæ of the alder, and though I am given to understand that in this stage the alder passes the greater part of its existence in the black mud formed by decaying vegetation, I made a sort of imitation of them which rather pleased me, and I tried it in Germany in mid-May. Whether the trout are or are not familiar with the natural insect in this stage I cannot say, but they took the imitation with such avidity that I speedily wore out my three specimens. They were only made as an experiment, and I tried no more, as I felt qualms in my mind as to whether it was quite the game to imitate this insect in this stage, any more than it would be to fish an imitation of the caddis. I am therefore not giving my recipe. Nor do I give that for making a caddis or gentle which I once tried, with mad success for a few minutes, and gave up, conscience-stricken. I have since seen alder larvæ in a glass tank in the Insect House at the Zoological Gardens, and, though their conditions are there no doubt quite artificial, they were swimming so freely and seemed so much at home in the water that I think it more than probable that they venture into the open often enough to be familiar to the trout. The long pale trailing processes along their sides suggested to me whether there was not to be found in the alder larvæ the prototype of the bumble.

I was at one time greatly interested in an attempt to imitate the fresh-water shrimp, and I tied a variety of patterns, including several with backs of quill of some small bird dyed greenish-olive, and ribbed firmly while wet and impressionable with silk or gold wire; but somehow I never used or attempted to use any one of them. I, however, gave one to an acquaintance, and he tied it on, and, standing on a footbridge, cast it downstream over some trout which were reputed uncatchably shy. At the first cast a big fish rushed at the shrimp, slashed it, and went off leaving the one-time owner lamenting.

CHAPTER V

SPECIAL CONDITIONS AND WET-FLY SOLUTIONS

NERVES.

YEARS ago, long ere the spirit of revolt was in me, when I followed as closely as I knew how the maxims of the apostles of the dry fly, and knew no other method for chalk streams, I suffered many blank days and much depression from a state of weather and light which must be familiar to all chalk-stream anglers—the more particularly because the "d——d good-natured" and sympathetic friend who knows nothing of the subject picks it out to say knowingly: "What a beautiful day for fishing!" It is clouded, dull, leaden, overhung, and the reflected light on the water is a dead milk-and-watery white; while, looking down into its depths, one sees everything with a deadly and crystalline clearness. There is no hint of thunder about, but on such days the trout are all nerves. Never are they so difficult to approach, never are they so ready to dart off with that torpedo wave. And if one finds a rising fish, and puts a dry fly over him, even if he bolts not, he rises no more.

But at length there came a day when my first timid experiments in the fishing of chalk streams with the wet fly had proved encouraging enough to lead to my having a small stock of wet-fly patterns for chalk-stream fishing. It was a bad sample of those days when the nerves of trout seemed all on the jump, and I had fished from 10 a.m. to 3 p.m. without so much as a rise. It was not that the fish were not rising. On the contrary, they rose very well—not very much, perhaps, but the best days are often those when the rise is moderate. But this day every fish I cast to went down at once, and too often I saw that detestable torpedo wave, sometimes at the approach, and more frequently at the first cast.

Soon after three I tied on a Tup's Indispensable dressed on gut, and crawled carefully to within a long cast of a trout which rose at infrequent intervals in a narrow side-stream under the opposite side. My line trailed on the water as I approached, and I made the minimum of effort to dry the fly ere I delivered it, so as to attract as little attention as possible to my movements. So it came about that the fly, when it lit a yard or more to the left of and above the trout—it was a bad cast as regards direction—went under immediately. For the nth time that day I saw that torpedo wave as the fish darted through the shallow water. I rose with a sigh, but as I did so my rod was a hoop, and the reel screeched: for the trout's dart had been *at* the fly, not from it, and it had gone a full yard or more to fetch it. He was just short of one and three-quarter pounds. Before four o'clock I had another brace by the same method. They were not easy, and I did not get every fish I tried, or even many; but I got some where with the dry fly I should assuredly have gone on getting none, and the trout stood to be cast to in a way they would not that day to the dry fly.

It is true enough that there are days and times when the dry fly will beat the wet fly hollow, but there are days when the converse is the case, and from subsequent experience I can recommend the trial of the wet fly on those dull, nervy days of milk-and-watery glare.

OF THE TROUT OF GLASSY GLIDES.

There are places on most rivers where the water comes swiftly and in solid volume down a slope too slight in the incline to create a fall, too short to create a rapid or stickle, and too smooth to cause a broken surface, yet with a rapid run below. The result is a glassy glide, gin-clear, with an air of unusual smoothness, and such a pace that there is an immediate drag upon any floating fly which is laid upon the current. Often some of the handsomest and best fighting trout in the river are to be found in such places, where their blood is constantly refreshed by the highly oxygenated water, their health and energy kept up to the mark by the need of contending against its swiftness, and the inducement to so contend is present in the plentiful supply of food brought down by the current.

Such a glide do I know well, with some excellent fish always showing there, but never breaking the surface; and for years I found them impregnable, for the simple reason that, if one pitched a fly over their noses, it was past them before they could rise to it, and if one pitched it up enough to give the fish a chance to take it they wouldn't, because there was a prompt and streaky drag if the line were, as it could hardly help being, the least little bit across stream. Even the natural fly would sail over them unmolested.

But one day some years back, on a calm afternoon in July, with not a trout rising, I was on the Itchen, and I had crawled up some half-mile of sedgy bank in search of a feeding fish without finding one. But on the far side, in front of a certain post, the remnant of a one-time fence, I knew from experience that there was usually a fish—at any rate at feeding-time. There was nothing to suggest any particular dry fly, and on the previous afternoon— a Sunday—I had spent a pleasant twenty minutes watching a fish in front of the stump taking something under water with a sort of porpoise roll. It therefore occurred to me to put up one of those little Greenwell's Glories, dressed by Forrest of Kelso on pairs of No. 00 hooks to gut, with which the name of Mr. Ewen M. Tod is associated. I had bought them in the previous spring to experiment upon bulging trout. These flies are known as "doubles," and are not ready floaters. One puts a thumb-nail between the barb, and forces them apart till the two hooks form an angle of 45 degrees with each other. The fly dropped a yard above the post and sank. When it should have been nearing the post, a faint swirl rising to the surface seemed a sufficient indication of a movement below to justify a raising of the rod-point, and the fish was fast. In this manner it came about that a small Greenwell's Glory on double hooks terminated the cast when the glassy glide above adverted to was reached. A trout lay out in it in position to feed, but though he moved a little from side to side, and may have been intercepting food, he made no rise. Keeping well out of sight, I dropped the Glory on the far side of and in front of the fish, and it at once went under. Again came the small disturbance welling quickly to the surface; up went my hand, and again a good trout was fast.

That afternoon I killed two and a half brace of good fish with the wet fly fished into likely places without seeing a single rise. The other three fish—but that is another story.

Since that day I have killed many a good fish in that hitherto impossible spot, and one morning in July, 1908, I had two and a half brace out of it in less than an hour with a wet double Tup's Indispensable.

OF THE WET FLY IN POOLS, BAYS, AND EDDIES.

There is probably no problem which has filled the souls of so many dry-fly anglers with the despair attending defeat as that presented by a day when a cross-stream wind, whether up and across, down and across, or straight across, drives every dun under the opposite bank, and into little pools and eddies between the prominences on that bank, and so out of the line of the current which would otherwise carry them along. Then every big trout in the river seems to shift out of the current and into the sheltered bay or eddy, and there he sets to work collecting with busy neb the little argosies which have lost their tide, and are drifting helpless on slack water. It seems so easy to drop the fly in the right place. So it is, but if, as is many times more than probable, your cruiser is away a foot or two, or is deliberate in his movements, and does not take the fly at once, your drag has made itself painfully evident, and your fish is down for half an hour. No, on those occasions the only chance with the dry fly is to hit your fish with it on the tip of the nose at a moment when few natural flies are about. Then he may snap it—but what a number of chances against its so falling!

No, here is a case in which the wet fly is clearly predicted, and it should be so dressed as to go under without the least hesitation. The advantage which the wet fly has is not that the trout is taking the nymph in preference to the floating dun, though he is probably doing that far more than is apparent, but that, whereas a drag on the surface is fatal and betrays the gut, an underwater drag is not betraying, and the movement of the fly caused by the drag may, in its beginning at any rate, be even attractive to the trout, as imparting motion suggesting life and volition to an otherwise suspicious object. The drag also serves to tighten instead of slackening the line, so that a very small strike fixes the hook.

When the trout takes a wet fly in such a position, the surface indications are by no means obvious; but if the angler be on the alert to strike when such indications come, it is wonderful how soon he can pick up the knack, and what excellent fish this method brings him. A strike which does not touch the fish, being in the nature of an under-water drawing of the fly, will often have no scaring effect upon a feeding fish, where a strike with a floating fly would send him headlong to cover.

It is difficult to pick among my recollections one instance more illustrative than another of the value of this method, but I will take an afternoon in July, 1908. It was a cold day for the time of year, with a keen north-westerly wind across and a little down. A few little pale duns were going down, being beaten by the wind

SPECIAL CONDITIONS AND WET-FLY SOLUTIONS

into and among the bays along the opposite bank, where they dodged in and out among the flags. Three trout, and three only, could I find moving, and they were taking every dun which went over them. I tried Little Marryat, Medium Olive, Flight's Fancy, Ginger Quill, and Red Quill, in vain. In fact I put all three down. But they meant feeding, and were soon going again. It was the last day of a seven-day visit. I had so far forty-six trout, and I wanted to round off the fifty. I put up as an experiment a tiny dotterel hackle, tied with primrose tying silk in the true Stewart style, not with the fibres radiating from the head, but palmerwise for halfway down the body. The trout had it at the very first offer, and was duly landed. I went on to the next, and got him almost immediately. The third, for some reason, had no use for Dotterel duns, but the moment I covered him with a Tup's Indispensable he slashed it, and joined the other two in my creel. I looked in vain for a fourth, and there was no evening rise, so I had to leave off with but forty-nine of my fifty. But for the wet fly, I am convinced I should have had to content myself with the single brace which the morning rise had brought me, and that would have been a disappointing ending to a good seven days.

OF THE JUDICIOUS USE OF THE MOON.

Though blinder than the proverbial bat in any slanting light, and therefore not as fortunate as I should like to be in fishing the evening rise, and though academically of opinion that fishing should cease when the dusk no longer lets the angler discern his fly, I confess to being at least as unwilling as any better endowed with sight to leave the water-side while the trout are still busy sucking down the spinners; but there are occasions when, if the moon be up enough to cast black shadows under the banks, and I can find the suitable spot with rising fish, I envy no man his superior eyesight—mine is good enough. Let me illustrate my meaning by describing the occasion on which I made my little discovery.

It was an evening in July. I had not begun fishing before four o'clock, and the afternoon had only earned me a single trout, and he no great shakes, either. The evening rise came on, and the trout began to feed briskly; but my infirmity was against me, and I missed or misjudged several rises, and it began to look as if I were going to make nothing of my opportunity, when I came to a bend where the current swung in pitch-black shadow under the opposite bank, while between the near edge of the shadow and my bank the stream ran molten moonlight. Round the bend in the dark I could hear the trout feeding away gaily, and the rings of their rises surged into the silver of the lighted current.

It seemed a mad thing to do, but I despatched my Tup's Indispensable to a spot in the dark as near as I could judge above the ring of a good fish. My cast lay like a hair on the surface, stretching into the dark, not too taut. Suddenly I saw my gut draw straight upon the current, the farther end disappearing under the sheen of the moonlight, and, without waiting to think, I raised my rod-point, to find myself in battle with a solid fish. Thrice in the twenty minutes the rise lasted did I repeat this experience. Each trout was soundly hooked, and a nice level lot they were, running from one and a quarter to one and a half pounds. Thus was success at the last moment pulled by a fluke out of almost certain defeat. It is not always possible to find place and light serving in this way, but if you do, make use of the moon.

THE WET-FLY OIL TIP.

In my observations upon the judicious use of the moon, I indicated the advantage to be derived, in cases where the light prevented the rise from being otherwise detected in due time, from watching the gut cast as a float signalling the taking of the fly. Indeed, it is not only by night that the cast may be watched with advantage, but often by day when casting a fly, wet or dry, but especially wet, into a bad light, while the cast or part of it may be seen floating on a glassy piece of water. It is now some years since, in the columns of the *Fishing Gazette*, I called attention to what I described as the "wet-fly oil tip" in this connection. I take no credit for this invention. It belongs entirely to Mr. C. A. M. Skues, the secretary of the Fly-fishers' Club, and its discovery came about in this way :

We were fishing opposite banks of a German trout stream, the Erlaubnitz, and the day rise of fly was over. The trout, which had been hovering over their pockets in the weeds and in the runs between them, had dropped out of sight, and it was obvious that it would need to attract them something more noticeable than the pale watery duns which were the staple of the season. We agreed upon Soldier Palmers tied with bright scarlet seal's fur. Presently the far bank began catching them, though he was fishing upstream wet in rather fast water. I hailed him, and he said he had paraffined his gut cast to within the last two links from the fly and watched his cast. I was not above a hint, and in a minute or two I was experiencing the benefit of the wet-fly oil tip, and we were kept busy till six o'clock brought on the usual rise of Little Pale Blue of Autumn, and a change to floating patterns. It also involved a change of cast, for a cross-stream cast with oiled gut betrays you with a vile drag. It is a disadvantage of paraffining your gut that it limits you to one cast— viz., that directly upstream. But there are times when it is well to accept the limitation.

OF GENERALSHIP AND THE WET FLY.

There is a bend on Itchen where the water runs deep and black. Over the best of it hang three large trees, under which, if trout be rising anywhere on the river, they will be found pegging away, and often when they are moving nowhere else. The place is near the spot where anglers foregather for lunch and a pull at pipe or flask; so the fish under these trees are hammered more than a little, and their knowledge is in direct proportion to their experience. Here, too, anglers usually take apart their split canes in the evening, and, ere they do so, have one last chuck in the dusk with Sedge, Coachman, or large Red Quill at one or all of these rising trout, but it is the rarest thing for one to be caught. I have caught six of them in fifteen years. Perhaps it is because to cover them one must fish straight across from the opposite bank—no other attack is possible—and they can hardly fail to see rod and angler.

But it fell about in the year of grace 1909 that my lawful occasions took me along the right bank, on which the trees grew, past the haunt of these aggravating risers, and I took the occasion to observe. None of them were moving at the time, and the water was lower by some inches than the normal. I looked in the place where the best of the risers was usually present when attending to business, but he was not there. Four or five yards farther upstream the bottom, from being shallow, dipped suddenly to the deep, with a sharp brown earthy edge; and there, lying in shelter from the current under the earthy ledge at the head of the hole, lay a trout which I put down at a comforting two pounds. He saw me, and slithered into his fastness, but I did not forget the hint. Many times had I cast to that trout when rising, but always under a tree some yards below. Now I would cast to him when not rising, and I would fish him in his hide. The lowest of a small cohort of ribbon-weeds craning their tips gently over the surface indicated the neighbourhood of the lip of the hole, and, scanning the opposite side carefully, I marked the exact bunch of yellow flower from behind which I ought to deliver my cast, and marked on the hither bank a bunch of purple hemlock which indicated the centre of the hole.

Later in the day from the opposite bank I sent over a wet

SPECIAL CONDITIONS AND WET-FLY SOLUTIONS

Tup's Indispensable to the weed's edge several times without avail.

The next time I came down the fish was rising to surface food, and I left him severely alone. My time was to be when he was not rising, for no trout seems able to resist a nymph at any time, even if not feeding, and a nymph of sorts he should have. Coming back later, I found stillness reigning; so, mounting a Tup's Indispensable, I soaked it well, and flicked it over to the edge of the weeds. It lit, and went under, leaving the gut for the most part along the surface. The gut drifted down, the fly end slowly slipping under the upper film. The fly was withdrawn and the cast repeated. Once more the gut lay along the surface; once more it slipped slowly through to a point; then it seemed to move under with a certain decision. I raised my rod-point with a drawing action, and the trout which had defied ten thousand dry flies was on. He wasn't quite two pounds, but it doesn't matter. It was generalship which got him, which discerned that in his holt he was possibly accessible to the seductions of the casual nymph-suggesting wet fly in a way in which he was not accessible to the temptations of the too well known dry fly in the place of vantage where he daily fed.

A POTTED TROUT, AND ONE OTHER.

When the drowners are out in the water-meadows flushing the ditches till they flood the tables and drench the grasses with water seeeking its way back through the herbage to the river by way of ditch, drain, and carrier, the wise old trout who know their business may be found in narrow ditches and channels down to foot-wide runnels in search of the earthworm and the miscellaneous pickings of the grasslands. Again, when July comes round, and the season of minnowing is indicated, the big trout once more make their way, in search of minnows, into the narrower irrigation channels of the water-meadows. So ardent are they at times in pursuit of their quarry that on occasion it is possible to net them out without their becoming aware of their danger.

On one occasion I got three good trout thus from behind at one scoop of the landing-net, and turned them back into the main.

Often, if they get into a channel with a constant flow and a steady food-supply, trout will not care to drop back to the river, and will take up a position of strength, where, inaccessible to the fly of the angler, they daily increase in size and lustihood. Such potted fish are almost entirely subaqueous feeders, a floating dun rarely crossing their field of vision. They grow dark and copper-coloured, and very unlike the fish of the river from which they hail.

One such fish do I remember, who took up his holt in the eddy just above a hatch-hole, through which ran the whole of a brisk stream some two to two and a half feet wide, turning at right angles to do so, after impinging on his eddy as on a sort of water-buffer. It was not hard to approach the place without being seen, but the moment one looked over the edge his troutship would flash down through the hatch-hole and into the racing stream beneath. Several times I mounted a Sedge, tied on a No. 2 hook attached to a strong cast, and dibbed cautiously over the edge. Once I caught a companion trout of one pound five ounces, but on all other occasions the attempt was fruitless.

Tired at length of these failures, and not pleased that such a trout as our friend of the hatch-hole eddy should give no sport to the fly, one afternoon I approached the hatch-hole from below, slid down my wide and large landing-net into the thrust of the stream, and looked suddenly over into the eddy. There was a brown flash to the hole, and next moment the trout was kicking in the net—black hogback with red copper sides and gleaming white belly, two and a half pounds, and as fat as a pig. Swiftly I conveyed him the needful fifty yards or so to a side-stream some ten or twelve yards wide, and turned him carefully loose. He made no pretence of being scared, but moved leisurely away across and up stream. I watched him cross a patch of weeds and enter a gravelled clearing, where a tidy trout lay, butt him out of it, and establish himself in his place. In a few moments he moved up into the next place, butted out the brace of trout which occupied it, and took the position of vantage. He did not remain long, but moved to the next pool, again ejecting the occupants.

Still dissatisfied, he moved higher up to where the stream was narrowed by camp-sheathing to support a low wooden bridge over which carts pass to carry the meadow hay. Here he ejected the three or four occupants, and established himself finally, with his neb close up under the sill of the bridge—too close for a fly to be got in ahead of him—obviously with the key of the larder in his pocket; and here daily for the next five days of my stay I saw him firmly planted, but, though I plied him with Sedge, and Quill, and Tup's Indispensable, wet fly and dry fly, I never got an offer or an indication of a desire to offer from him, nor did I ever see him break the surface, and I left him *in situ* at the end of my visit.

During these five days, however, crossing from the smaller stream to the main, I saw a trout in a foot-wide runnel hovering with that quivering of the fins that indicates a willingness to feed. He was not a big fish—about one pound—but I thought it would be sport to try and cast to him and catch him in so narrow a channel, and I knelt down to deliver the fly. He saw me, however, and moved up. It was on my way 'cross meadow to the main, so I followed him till I came to the place where the runnel's water-supply issued from a pipe which entered its head, at right angles to its course, from the centre of one of the tables. The flow from the pipe had worried out a corner hole, which was wide and deep enough to admit my whole landing-net and a bit over, and I dipped it in. I saw the amber gleam of my trout as he slashed by me and fled back down the runnel he had ascended, but wriggling in the net which I lifted was a bouncing fish, black, hogbacked, with copper sides and white belly, in first-rate fettle, and weighing better, at a guess, than one and a half pounds, evidently an old inhabitant of that corner. The main was but a few yards off, and I carefully turned in my captive.

Two days later I was fishing up the bank of the main in blazing sunshine, searching for a rising fish, but finding none, when my attention was attracted by a movement in the water close under my bank some ten or fifteen yards above the spot where I turned the trout in. I dropped my wet Greenwell's Glory a foot or so from the spot, and, answering the draw of the floating gut signalling some under-water adhesion, I tightened on a nice fish, and after the usual preliminary exhibition of coyness, emphasized by sundry jumpings, he was persuaded to come ashore. The spring-balance said one pound ten ounces. Colour, size, and shape, were identical with the trout I had turned back two days before, and though, of course, I cannot prove it, I have no doubt he was the same.

Now, why did one of these potted trout take the fly, and the other refuse? This is my theory: Both had got the exclusive habit of subaqueous feeding, but the big one had his nose in a position where it was impossible to get a wet fly to him so as to pitch above him, or even alongside of his head, and the water was too fast for it to be worth the while of a fish of his calibre to turn and follow a mere nymph. The smaller fish was in a position to be covered, and the moment the nymph came to him under water he had it as a matter of course. Possibly, in the same position the larger trout might have done the same.

OF TWO SATURDAY AFTERNOONS.

They were consecutive. Both were in August, 1909, and the reason why they are recorded is not because of any remarkable

SPECIAL CONDITIONS AND WET-FLY SOLUTIONS

success, but because they illustrate varying conditions on the same river, proving amenable to varying treatment.

The first found me by the water-side soon after two o'clock. The morning rise was completely over. Not even a grayling was rising. The water was deadly still. A full stream was running, because the hay-makers were in the meadows, and no water that could be kept out was being let into ditches and carriers; so it was no good exploring them for stray risers, as at other times I might have done. For some time I explored likely places under the sedges with floating flies—No. 1 Red Sedge with hare's-ear body, Red Ant, and Tup's Indispensable—but without eliciting the faintest response. Then about five o'clock I put up a wet Greenwell's Glory, and cast it upstream, wet, into every little likely pool between the bank and the weed-bed which grew intermittently a yard or two out from the bank. The change was immediate. By six o'clock I had three and a half brace of average fish (biggest one pound ten ounces), all on the same fly. Fish would surge a yard or more to meet it, would even turn downstream and take it, though the floating fly had not moved a single one to offer. There was no evening rise.

The following Saturday I was down at the same time. There was the same faint westerly breeze, and much the same light. A few—very few—grayling were taking black gnats for a short time after my arrival, but they soon stopped entirely, and I had only one in my basket. Not a rise dimpled the surface. I continued, however, casting a Black Gnat under my own bank—the right—for some forty or fifty yards, without an offer. I had the mortification of seeing three handsome trout move out from position, and I was just about to change to a Hare's Ear Sedge when I saw a grassmoth flutter out of the serges and across the water. As luck would have it, I had four floating Grannom in my cap, and it didn't take long to knot one on.

In a few minutes I was into a trout, which took as the fly lit. I landed him, and then another, and yet a further brace, every one of which took the Grannom without the least hesitation. Then I found myself trenching on the beat of another angler, and I bethought me that the three fish I had disturbed might be back in position; so I turned down, and, getting below them, cast carefully to where they ought to be. I whipped one fly off; then with the new fly I rose the first of them—quite a nice fish—hooked him, and lost him after a short tussle. Examining the hook, I found it pulled out nearly straight owing to a soft wire. Whether that rattled me or not I don't know, but I left my two remaining Grannom in the other two fish successively. Having no more, I fell back on the Sedge in vain. Equally vain were Red Ant (dry) and Greenwell's Glory and Tup's Indispensable (wet), and, as there was no evening rise, I finished up with a basket of two and a half brace, which with better handling should have been four brace.

On each of these afternoons there was no rise of fish or fly; and on one nothing but a floating pattern did any good, on the other nothing but a sunk pattern.

The inference that I might have gone back blank on the first occasion but for the supplemental aid of the wet-fly method does not seem far-fetched.

CHAPTER VI

UNCLASSIFIED

OF HOVERING AND SOARING, AND OF CRUISING TROUT.

THE trout that is glued to the bottom is generally a pretty hopeless fish. He is either not willing to feed, or, being willing, his suspicions have been aroused and he has gone down. Pretty stories are told of how such fish are occasionally startled into taking by the fly being slammed down with violence on or just behind their heads, but no such instance has come within my experience.

But the trout which is hovering in mid-water or near the surface is always a hopeful subject. Anglers will tell you he is willing to feed. In my belief, he is more than that; he is generally actively feeding—under water.

I remember a trout which lay in the same hole with six grayling. He was hovering not far below the surface, but would have nothing to say to a series of dry flies of appropriate pattern offered him; but a wet Greenwell's Glory was too much for him, and he turned and took it first cast. He was undoubtedly feeding on nymphs, but not over weed, and so not bulging; yet he presented only the appearance of hovering, or, as Walton generally calls it, "soaring."

Another likely fish is the cruiser on his way to his feeding-station. If I see a wedge-shaped ripple advancing irregularly upstream, and broken at times by a dimple in the centre, I always feel hopeful, and I know that the trout which cause these are nearly always of unusual size for the water. It is, of course, difficult to place the fly exactly; but if that difficulty is overcome, your trout will take it most unsuspiciously. The best course is to throw to one side and a little ahead of the last rise.

A more difficult proposition is the cruiser who has a small defined beat. You find him moving up the bank in such wise that every cast is short of his rise; but suddenly, if you are not ware, you will find that he has turned and sailed down-stream to the bottom of his beat, and that your rod and line are absolutely over him. Such a trout seems always fastidious and picksome, but it is all the more gratifying to circumvent him. He is usually taking toll of insects collected in eddies, and a spinner of sorts is more likely to take him than a dun; but he will often rush for a fly that is being withdrawn under water.

OF THE PORPOISE ROLL.

There is one peculiarity irritating kind of rise in which trout indulge. Just like porpoises, they come up, and, scarcely breaking the surface with the head, expose first the back fin and then the tail as they go down. Often of an afternoon or evening it seems as if every trout in the river were busy at this game. The difficulty is to know, on such occasions, what they are taking. "Detached Badger" (p. 119 of "Dry-Fly Fishing") suggests larvæ, but though at times I have caught fish thus rising with sunk flies, I am inclined to doubt their taking nymphs or larvæ, and to suspect spinners.* This (even if the trout be taking nymphs) is not properly described as "bulging," that term being confined to the swashing rises when a fish rushes to and fro, making visible waves, ending in a boil as it turns in the act of fielding the subaqueous insect. Fortunately, this porpoise type of rise is comparatively rare, for when trout indulge in it sport is consistently bad. -I have

* Generally spinners are indicated, but occasionally nymphs. See chapter on Assorted Rises, p. 89 of "The Way of a Trout with a Fly."

been promising myself for the last two or three seasons that, when I drop on such a rise, I will try Mr. F. M. Halford's spent spinner patterns, but in an average number of days' fishing I have failed to drop on an occasion when the trout have been thus rising.

CHAPTER VII

SUNDRY CONSIDERATIONS

OF THE RELATION OF PATTERN TO THE POSITION OF TROUT, AND HEREIN OF THE TAKING OFF OF WARY WILLY.

It is perhaps a small matter which is treated under this head, but anything which helps the angler to a correct selection of fly is so much to the good, and the point I want to make here is that the haunt of a fish is an item to be taken note of in deciding what items to put upon the menu to be offered for his selection. For instance, if your trout be in position in the middle of a fairly wide stream, and that be his habitual post, it is practically little good giving him an imitation of any insect which haunts the bank only, such as alder in its season, sedge, grass-moth, or willow-fly, which, on the other hand, may be tried in their season, with every prospect of success, upon fish under the banks.

Well do I remember how marked this rule was in its application on a day in September, 1903, on a German limestone river. In the middle the willow-fly, which was out in quantity that day, was no good. The trout wanted duns, and willow-flies were no use to them, or probably there, away from the banks, were practically unknown; but under the alder and willow-fringed banks on either side the trout took the spent willow-fly freely, and, of thirty-seven trout, no less than thirty-four fell that day to the willow-fly under the banks, but not one from mid-river. Many a time the trout will take a sedge or an imitation of the grassmoth under the banks when quite shy of them in midstream. In this connection I may record an incident which is framed in my mind as the strange disappearance of Wary Willy.

Wary Willy was almost a public character. He inhabited a club water not far from Winchester, and was always at his post when duty called. But he was of an obliging turn of mind, and always ready to show sport to the new-comer who might be tempted to put a fly over him. Yet it was not for nothing that he had earned his name, for, though many had risen him, none was recorded as having hooked him. His holt was under a grassy bank (right of the river), about three yards above the spot where a willow stump extended a solitary branch at right angles to the current, a foot above and about two yards out into the stream, so that any angler who paid his respects to William had to send his invitation across the willow-bough, a state of things which led to difficulties and language for the angler, and to an amused retreat on the part of Willy. Yet a short time later he would be back at his post, adding to his collection of the Ephemeridæ with undiminished zest.

I was not a member of the club, but I paid a visit to a friend who had a rod, and he very good-naturedly insisted on my trying his nine-foot Leonard over Wary Willy, and he brought me to the place. I had no tackle with me, so I had to use my friend's floating flies. The wind was light and in the right direction, and I got my fly over the branch nicely and covered him several times, and as I let my reel-line drop on the water below the branch the current carried my fly back successfully a number of times; but at length I was hung up, and when I tried to release myself Willy had business elsewhere.

On this water the club members and the keepers said that sedges were no use. It was a dun and spinner water only. So when in the afternoon I met the head-keeper, and saw a small Red Sedge in his cap, I made no bones of asking for it, as it was of no use. Borrowing the Leonard once more, I tied on the Red Sedge, and stole up cautiously to Willy's abode. But just ere I got to position a fish rose to the right of his place, about three yards out from the bank. I did not wish him to scare Willy, so, to get him out of the way first, I dropped the sedge upon his nose, and he had it immediately. He was very indignant at the imposition that had been put upon him, and turned several somersaults in the air, and altogether put up quite a good fight for a fish of his ounces, which numbered twenty-five, before my friend's landing-net received him. I had, however, steered him carefully, so that his antics should not disturb William, and I approached that worthy's holt with a modest confidence that William stood in the way of getting a surprise: But William was not there. William never came back. He couldn't. He was dead, and in my friend's landing-net. But it was several days before remorse began to work in me, for it was not till a week or so later that my friend told me of the disappearance of Wary Willy. But Willy had always been fished with duns. He knew all the patterns of Holland and Chalkley and Ogden Smith, but never had he had cause to suspect the genuineness of a sedge—and so, good-bye Willy!

OF THE USE OF SPINNERS DURING THE RISE OF DUNS, AND HEREIN OF THE VAGARIES OF THE BLUE-WINGED OLIVE.

"The Red Quill," says Mr. F. M. Halford, "is one of the sheet-anchors of the dry-fly fisherman on a strange river when in doubt." Never was a truer word spoken. Mr. Englefield of Winchester, I believe, conducted the experiment of confining himself to the Red Quill (in a variety of sizes and shades, and with and without the addition of gold and silver tags) for a whole season, and did as well with the one fly as in other seasons with a larger selection. And it is a remarkable fact that the Red Quill, bearing more resemblance to a Red Spinner than to a dun, will frequently kill during a rise of duns as well as, or better than, quite a good imitation of the dun itself. It will also be found that during the rise of any kind of dun its spinner will often take as well as, if not better than, the subimago pattern. For instance, a Red Spinner during a rise of olives, a Claret Spinner when the iron-blue dun is on, and a Sherry Spinner when the blue-winged olive is on.

All the spinners do not die and fall spent on the water over night. Some come on to the water in the cool of the early morning, and if the angler tries in the hot weather for an early morning trout, the spinner may be commended to him as giving him his best chance, so far as floating patterns are concerned. And when, before the rise comes on, an odd fish or so may be found in position putting up occasionally at something, spinners may legitimately be suspected. Therefore it may be that, when the rise comes on, the memory of a recent acquaintance with more delicious morsels than the current duns leads to a readiness on his part to absorb the floating imitation spinner.

The blue-winged olive is a large and handsome fly, and its hatch is usually an evening matter, though I have seen it at all hours of the day. But when it is on, and there are other duns at the same time, it is always possible to distinguish the trout which are taking the blue-winged olive by the curious shape of the boil they make in taking it; a kidney-shaped boil, with two distinct whorls right and left. And if the angler is provided with Orange Quills on No. 1 hooks, and will pick out these fish, he may count on sport worth remembering, though possibly not a spinner may be on the water at the time. Curiously enough, such a thing as a good imitation of the blue-winged olive in the subimago form has yet to be invented. Patterns are tied which will kill an occasional trout, but the Orange Quill, if the rise be anything like a good one, means three or four brace, and probably all big fish.*

One evening, June 24 in 1908, I ran down to Winchester by the 6.50 train to see Eton v. Winchester on the next day, and I got down there about eight o'clock. I had not meant to fish overnight, but I thought there was time for a cast before the dusk

* See chapter on the B. W. O., p. 176 of "The Way of a Trout with a Fly."

drew in, and I picked up a nine-foot Leonard and a landing-net, stuck a damper with a cast in it and a small box of flies in my pocket, and got down to a broad shallow. I found several fish rising, and at once diagnosed the blue-winged olive. So I tied on a large Orange Quill and cast to the nearest. Up he came, and was off with a flounder. Without losing a moment, I covered the next with the ensuing cast. The same thing occurred, and I promptly dropped my next cast a yard to the right over the third fish. He, too, came up and fastened. He went straight to weed, but, holding him quite lightly, I soon had the satisfaction of feeling him beat himself free of the weeds, and presently I netted him out. The fly was quite soaked, and I tried to change it, but it was too dark, and so I knocked off, having risen three trout to the Orange Quill in three successive casts.

Some years ago I dressed for my friend, M. Louis Bouglé, of Paris and the Fly-fishers' Club, a winged imitation of the blue-winged olive, which is at certain seasons almost the only dun on the chalk streams of Normandy, and he can kill an occasional fish on it. Its dressing is immaterial, for I never could do any good with it myself; but one evening I was fishing the Varennes with M. Bouglé, when there came on a good fall of blue-winged olive spinner. My friend caught a trout with his pattern, and by the aid of a spoon I got from its stomach, and turned into a glass, three large greenish-amber spinners, with the distinctive three setæ; and next morning in a capital light I tied an imitation of these insects, spent-gnat-wise, with seal's fur body of palish yellow-green olive of appropriate mixture of furs. Next evening we each got fish with these imitations, M. Bouglé more than I, and I have always been promising myself that I will put it up one blue-winged olive evening on the Hampshire rivers; but when the occasion has come, and that distinctive rise is seen, I have never been able to resist taking the Orange Quill rather than the spent olive pattern out of the box where they repose together. It is hard to resist three or four brace.

SUNDRY CONSIDERATIONS

OF GENERAL FEEDERS, AND HEREIN OF THE UNDOING OF AUNT SALLY.

There are places in most rivers—generally, I think, about the spots most frequented by man—where trout establish themselves, which seem, though willing enough to take duns as they come, to be independent of them as a staple food, and to take gaily every day and all day long, and often far into the night, whatever fly-food comes along, always excepting, *bien entendu*, the angler's flies, however delicately offered. Such trout are readily put off their feed, but not for long, and the angler, returning to the spot after a short absence, may make up his mind to find his friend back in position, pegging away as freely as ever. Everyone has a chuck at these fish—no one can resist them; but it is a rare thing for one to be caught—and the Coachman may account for a few. A strong ruffle in the water *may* enable you to take one unaware, but, generally speaking, the ordinary tactics, whether dry-fly or wet, are thrown away on such fish, and the only chance is to fall back on something exceptional either in lure or in method of attack, or both.

Followeth the example of

The Undoing of Aunt Sally.

She was called Aunt Sally because everyone felt bound to have a shy at her. Her coign of vantage was near the bottom of the water, where the fishery begins, and her irritating "pip, pip," as she took fly after fly in the culvert that was her home was too much for the nerves of nine anglers out of ten, so that the absurdest efforts to circumvent her were made daily—efforts to float a dry upwinged dun down the culvert from the top: result, immediate and irremediable drag; efforts to flick a fly upstream to her in the culvert from below: result, broken rod-tops, barbless hooks, flies flicked off against the brickwork, and other disasters, leading to profanity.

The *locus in quo* was a stream in the South of England, flowing some fifteen yards or so wide at a good even pace, with a nice purl on it, down to and past a deep hole used for bathing by the farmers' lads. From this hole, a culvert in the left bank, a yard wide and, say, four yards long, diverts a considerable body of the stream into a new channel, to drive a mill in the town below. This was the fastness in which Aunt Sally had taken up her abode, and throughout the spring and summer had defied all efforts to dislodge her.

It was my first visit to the stream that year, and from 9 a.m. till 3 p.m. on an August day I had worked away for meagre results. There was no rise of fly after ten o'clock, and a strong rise of water-rats. Three trout had I turned over, and one of one pound two ounces reposed in my bag. I had not seen a rising fish for hours, when, weary and disappointed, I drifted down the right bank to the bottom of the fishery, and sat down to rest on the steps which are set in the hole to assist bathers in clambering out.

"Pip!" I heard coming from somewhere. I looked upstream, I looked under my own bank, but not a sign of a ring was to be seen. "Pip, pip!" again. At last, leaning low and looking through the culvert, I saw, some two yards down, what I took to be a dimple of a rising fish. Watching a few moments, I saw it repeated, and my spirits revived. My point was fine, so I took it off and knotted on a yard of sound Refina gut, and ended it with a brown beetle with peacock's herl body and red legs. I soaked him well, so that there should be no drag on the surface, and then, getting my length for the other side, let the fly and gut drag in the stream till the moment I made my cast. Fly and gut together struck the brick face of the culvert, and fell in a heap at the mouth. Instantly the current caught the fly and gut, and extended them down the culvert. Almost at the same moment the current of the main stream, across which my reel-line lay, began to drag upon it, and completed the extension of the gut by the time the beetle had run a short two yards down the culvert. At once it began to drag back. This was too much for Aunt Sally—to have that beetle scuttling from her when it was almost in her mouth. She came at it, and in a flash secured it ere it could escape from the culvert; and before she could turn she was skull-dragged out of her fastness and turned down into the stream below. She made a determined fight for it, but she was very soundly hooked, and I gave no needless law, so that her fifteen inches were soon laid out upon the grass. Not knowing of her fame, I was quite content with her one pound eleven ounces; but an angler who told me of her reputation said she had always been put down as a much bigger fish. An hour later I looked down the culvert again, but the water had dropped some inches, and there was not enough current through the culvert to make it fishable. I had hit the happy moment for the undoing of Aunt Sally.

OF ATTENTION TO CASUAL FEEDERS.

The happening fish is a godsend to the angler whom time or trains, failure to find the taking fly, or other act of God or the King's enemies, have prevented from making his basket during the main hatch of duns. By the "happening fish" is to be understood, not the chance riser to a chance cast, but the trout which, by reason of a larger stomach capacity, misfortune of position, shortage of fly, disinclination for the society of tailers, or the pursuit of the succulent shrimp, or neglect of his opportunities during the main rise, is left hungry, or at least hungry enough not to have left off feeding after—often long after—the main rise has faded out; and also the trout whose hearty appetite ranges him under the bank in advance of the rise, in a state of impatience for his meal, which leads him to sample such *hors d'œuvres* as the stream may bring his way. For reasons which shall be made apparent, both of these classes of trout offer themselves an easier prey to the angler than the trout who is busy with a steady diet of hatching duns. It is doubtful whether the advice often tendered to the over-eager, to allow the rising trout to get well set at the wicket, is really sound, as, by the time he is well set, his appreciation of what is offered him has become greatly sharpened by a prolonged experience of it as it should be, and he is as likely as not to refuse anything that does not appeal to him as being identical with the natural insect he has been absorbing so much of; and I know no more likely fish to take, if you get your fly to him right, than a trout which is cruising up to his feeding-ground, picking a fly or two on the way. Freely I confess that whole rises have passed me too many á time without my having succeeded in ascertaining what the trout would take, and on such days—and again on days when trains have borne me to the water too late for the morning rise—I might frequently, but for my friend the casual feeder, have brought home a toom creel.

The places where the casual feeder is to be found at home are various; but, speaking generally, the casual feeder's position depends on the nature of the fare which the time of day affords him, and the odds are long that from the end of May, when the first of the sedges (the so-called Welshman's Button—the "Dun Cut" of the fathers of angling) comes upon the water, that position will be found under the banks where sedge-flies and other bank insects most do congregate, and from which they venture upon the water; at bridges where a constriction of the current concentrates the food; at bridges where spinners are apt to dance until their dancing minutes be done, and sedges often shelter in brickwork; at hatches where woodlice and other insects harbour in the wood, and are prone to drop into the current; in pockets in the weeds; and in ditches and carriers where the hatch of duns is sparse and unsatisfactory, and a trout must rely upon other resources for his daily sustenance. This may be floating or subaqueous, but is more likely in carriers and swift waters to be subaqueous, inasmuch as it is only for a brief period that a hatch takes place; but subaqueous forms of fly-life are always about (though, no doubt, sparsely at other times than that of the rise), and experience proves that when no definite rise is in progress, no trout that is on the alert finds it easy to resist a nymph who has left his shelter. Hence, given the willingness of the trout to feed, and the absence of a steady diet of dominant attractiveness, there is every inducement for him to be of an open mind as to the provender that will seduce him.

Then there is our friend the "tailer," of whom more elsewhere.

Thus, instead of spiking his rod when the morning rise is over, and taking his Walton or his Marcus Aurelius or his Omar Khayyám from his pocket, let the wise angler concentrate on the casual feeder; and if his reward be not great, there is every chance of its being quite respectable, and he may be saved the humiliation of an empty creel.

OF THE FREQUENTATION OF DITCHES, DRAINS, AND CARRIERS.

I know of no sight more gloomy than that of a golfer painfully tramping from shot to shot. But perhaps the next gloomiest sight is the angler who, with perhaps but a single day at his disposal, lounges hour by hour by the side of the main river, waiting with such patience as he can muster for the rise which comes not. Let us suppose that he is either unable or too magnanimous to fish the wet fly, that there are no fish lying, either visibly or inferentially, in convenient places under his own bank, so that they could be fished to with a dry sedge or a Red Quill. Let him come with me, and we will pull some sport out of adverse conditions. Let us begin here, where this hatch is letting a goodly supply of water into this carrier for the watering of the meadows. Be it known unto you, O angler, that the trout of ditches and carriers are far less affected by the rise of duns, and far readier to feed at all times or any time, than those fish of the main river. Here our choice is to fish either a sunk fly, suggesting a nymph (for here an upwinged dun can hardly get through undrowned), a floating fly resembling one of the sedges which dodge about the camp-sheathing or a good-sized Wickham's Fancy. Search all the tail of the run carefully with one or the other of these patterns, and it shall go hard with you if you do not get a chance, at any rate, from a passable fish—possibly more than one.

A little lower down the carrier runs through a culvert, and, if the hay-makers have not got him out, one is likely to find quite a respectable trout just below the arch, and he is to be had if you fish him right. Farther down there is a low wood bridge, through which the stream flows briskly, and below this there are usually two or three feeding fish. For some reason these are specially sensitive to shadow. I have had many fish from this spot from both sides, but never one from the right, or west, side after two o'clock, or from the other side before two. Having fished these fish, and caught or lost or put them down, let us move over to the next piece of water. It is slow, and has little weed. If it had been a day with a ruffle of wind, or had the drowners turned a good current through, we would have fished it up yard by yard; but to-day it is no good. But here, a bit farther on, a brisk stream runs through a little hatch, and for a hundred and fifty yards or so makes a most merry little length. Keep low in the long grass, fish it foot by foot, and, so far as you can, turn *down* all the fish you scare. If you send one up, sit down and wait. It will not be long ere the others recover their equanimity. On a good day you should get your two brace from this length, either with No. 1 Red Sedge, No. 1 Red Quill, No. 0 Pink Wickham or No. 0 Tup's Indispensable wet, or No. 0 Wickham's Fancy. Now let us wind up along another brisk little piece of water, perhaps fifteen feet wide, which races in a series of runs, and stretches right across the meadows. It is known as the Highland Burn, and it is full of sporting fish, and you must take the chance of hooking a half-pounder along with your chance of a fish nearer two pounds. And do not neglect the ditch which runs in at right angles halfway up. I have seen a past-master take no less than three capital trout from those few yards in one day, turning each as hooked down into the Highland Burn, and killing him there.

OF THE NEGOTIATION OF TAILERS.

Authority hath it that "the best policy is, perhaps, to leave tailing fish alone"; but the busy man, who only gets an occasional day's fishing, to whom that advice is too trying and disappointing (meaning me), was recommended to try an Orange Bumble or a Furnace. With an exception I shall presently refer to, it is some years since I have had any experience of tailing trout, for an alteration in a weir has made such a difference in the pace and level of a length on the chalk stream I most do fish, that whereas in the old days the tailer used to be a common sight there, nowadays it is the greatest rarity. But in those old days the tailer was my stand-by. If—as was frequently the case—I made naught of the morning rise, I would betake me to this length and sit down gaily to the siege of each tailer in succession, with the confidence that, unless I made some mistake and scared the fish—and tailers are not too easily scared—sooner or later he was my fish. It was often later, for I had to go on casting, casting, casting, in the hope that the moment might come when my fly would be passing over the trout at the moment when his head was raised, and he was taking breath before another big go at the shrimps and other food in the weed-beds. The frequent casting gave much opportunity for mistakes, and not infrequently I scared my fish, after wasting half an hour or more over him; but, on the other hand, I seldom failed to secure at least one fish, and oftener a leash. The method was simplicity itself. I sat down below my fish, and dropped a Pink Wickham a yard or so above where his tail dimpled the surface, and floated it down over him quite dry.

This was repeated so long as the fish was there, but if he lifted his head in time to see the fly come over him, there seemed to be some mysterious attraction in that pattern which forbade him to refuse it. Whether this is so in other waters I know not, but I often regret the obliteration of the old race of tailers. They were a great stand-by, and always put up a big battle when hooked. The size of fly was 00 for smooth water, but in a ruffle the single cipher size proved better medicine.

The single occasion above referred to was in May, 1909, in a different part of the river. The water was running thinly over a broad shallow, very full up with weed-beds, and, instead of standing nearly perpendicularly on their heads in order to tail, large numbers of trout and grayling were grubbing at an acute angle with the bottom among the weed-beds, and with violent wriggles of head and body dislodging small insects, which they pursued with rushes plainly marked upon the surface, ending, at the moment of capture of the prey, with swirls. I did not put up a Pink Wickham, because I had another experiment to make. In the previous July I had caught three brace before eleven o'clock on a nymph imitated in olive seal's fur from one found in the mouth of a trout on the previous day, and I wanted to give it a trial here, on the chance that it might be found that it was nymphs, and not shrimps, that the tailing fish were shaking out. So, keeping the artificial nymph soaking at the end of my line in the run at my feet, I despatched it every now and then across the course of the trout, when, desisting from their grubbing, they pursued the flying quarry. It was generally the case that, by the time the fly lit, the fish was careering off in some different direction; but several fish pursued my fly and swirled at it, and one takable trout and one short of the regulation twelve inches succeeded in taking it. It was a short and most inconclusive experiment, but, if occasion serves, it will be renewed.

SUNDRY CONSIDERATIONS

OF THE FASCINATION OF BRIDGES.

Years ago, before ever I knew the Upper Itchen, there was a wooden farm bridge which crossed the main river to carry produce. Whether the bridge fell into decay through disuse and neglect consequent upon the fields on the east side being separately let to another farmer, or whether the separate letting occurred because the bridge became dangerous, and would have cost too much to repair, at any rate, when I came to know this particular part of the river in the early eighties, there was nothing left of the bridge except a stump or two, green with slime, brown with rot, showing just above water, or intercepting weed—just that and a band of bottom a little higher than the river-bed above and below, as if the made bottom which had carried the bridge still persisted. Even the stumps are long gone the way of all stumps, and the made bed is only just traceable if you know where to find it. But for all that, after all these years, this is the place in the river where trout are to be found feeding, if they are found feeding anywhere; and they feed in much the same way, seeming secure, yet really shy, as the trout feed under or just below all the bridges on the river.* All bridge trout seem to be shy. Some bridges make shyer trout than others. I knew one—a railway-bridge on that length—under which in four-and-twenty years I never got a trout, or even a rise, for all I tried persistently, wet and dry, until 1908, and then only because on that particular day a strong ruffle of wind blew up the arch and made good big waves. Then I got a brace to a floating Tup's Indispensable, and lost another fish. Whether it is the holt into which to run at hint of danger, or the insects which haunt the woodwork, or the clear space of unweeded water in which to swim, or what not, bridges seem to have a special fascination for trout; and if the fly (preferably a small sedge) can be delicately

* This is still the case in 1923.

dropped over the fish as if it fell from the woodwork, the chances of getting him are much increased.

Trout seem specially watchful at bridges, and, if the water be not too fast, will turn to take a fly which is aimed to hit them on the tail.

CHAPTER VIII

MAINLY TACTICAL

OF THE DELIBERATE DRAG.

OF all trials of the chalk-stream angler, perhaps drag is the worst. Yet even drag may be made use of on occasion, to add to the weight of the creel. Years back, on the Erlaubnitz in South Germany, I sat by a mill-head on a blazing and wellnigh hopeless September afternoon. The water was low, much of the head having been run off by the sawmill, and such little current as there was confined itself almost entirely to the centre. Brown and dirty-looking weeds topped the surface along my side of the head. Suddenly I detected a tiny dimple in a little spot where, among the weeds, an eighteen-inch square of clean surface showed itself. I despatched my fly—a Landrail and Hare's Ear Sedge on a No. 3 hook—and by good luck or good management it dropped neatly on the spot. I waited. Three minutes passed. Nothing happened. Then I thought to recover my fly and drop it again in the hole, but with rather less delicacy, so as to attract attention to its fall. But first I had to recover it. I moved it gently towards the side of the hole, but I could not prevent the effect of a drag on the surface. Yet ere the fly had moved three inches a good pound-and-a-half trout had it, and, after a game of pully-hauly in the weeds, was duly brought to net. This was a limestone stream, and not a chalk stream.

But in August, 1908, I was on my way through the meadows to the main Itchen, when in a much-weed-encumbered carrier I became aware of a good trout lying in, and near the head of, a little pool of open water three or four yards long at most, and perhaps a third as wide. My rod and cast were ready, but no fly. So I knotted on a good big sedge—I think a No. 3 Silver Sedge. The water was glassy smooth, and the current would not have carried my fly the length of the open water in much under five minutes. I was afraid to cast above the fish, or to right or left of his head, for I knew it would send him scuttling to weed. I wanted to drop the fly just behind his eyes, but I misjudged, and it fell several inches short, almost upon his tail. I waited a moment; the trout lay still, but evidently excited. Then I remembered my German experience, and began to draw the fly along the surface. Immediately the trout turned and slashed it, and was soundly hooked. Candour compels me to admit that the gut was also smashed by a strike of unregulated violence; but this is entirely beside the point, for it in no sense detracts from the value of my illustration of the occasional serviceableness of the calculated drag on still waters, even with the dry fly.

My friend M. Bouglé acutely distinguishes drag of the kind here described as the drag of *déplacement*, as compared with the drag of *rétention*, which occurs on moving water.

On the Pang at Bradfield resides a blacksmith named Holloway, who is a first-rate angler, and I have seen him practise the deliberate drag on fast water with the May-fly in a manner which in other hands would send every trout scuttling to cover, but he did not put them down a bit. He ties a May-fly—not a very pretty confection, but admirably constructed for this purpose. The hackle, which is white, instead of standing out more or less at right angles to the hook-shank, is so tied as to lie almost flat upon it, and as a result the fly leaves practically no wake when it is drawn over the fish, and the movement, which he practises assiduously, far from scaring the fish, appears to be actually attractive. Yet the Pang fish are quite wary, and liberties may not be taken with them with impunity. In this case once more we have the drag of *déplacement*, but it is hard to see why it should not be just as fatal to the angler's chances as the drag of *rétention*.

IN THE GLASS EDGE.

A more unpromising May day than that I now tell of it would be hard to conceive. The wind—from the west, with a bite of north in it—blew for the most part dead across stream with strong, shuddering gusts, so violent at times as to force the angler, taken unawares, two or three steps nearer to the water's edge, and more than once nearly to precipitate him into the water between the sedgy tussocks which fringed one side of this length of Upper Itchen. On the previous day there had been a sparse skirmishing line of dark olives on the water at 10.15, covering the main advance at 11.30; but to-day 10.30, 11, 11.30, noon, and the intervening quarters, chimed from the belfry, without a fly showing on the water or in the air. At noon the sun shone out for a few moments, and made fitful reappearances at intervals till 1.30. Strolling slowly and watchfully up the bank, with an eye on the far side, the angler came upon Keeper Humphrey in attendance on another angler, and, on his advice, put up a Red Quill on a No. 0 hook, for lack of one a size larger, and, leaving the other a couple of hundred yards below, sat down to wait for the rise. At length a little upwinged dun was seen in sail in the glass edge, hugging the far bank as close as possible. For a few yards it staggered down, battered by the gale, and then slid sideways among the flags under pressure of a stronger gust than usual, and was lost to sight. Pitiably sparse the fly were, and in half an hour not more than half a dozen came in sight. All vanished disappointingly among the flags. But at last the watcher was rewarded by seeing one disappear in the centre of a tiny widening ring, which scarcely rippled out beyond the narrow glass edge. In a moment distance was got by a trial cast a yard or two downstream, and then the Red Quill dropped perkily a foot above the spot where the dun had disappeared, and went swiftly down on the full current—so swiftly that the angler did not realize until a second too late that the same neb which had lain in wait for the dun had sucked in the Red Quill. The strike was just too late, and a pricked and badly scared trout dashed violently out into the stream.

In' the next little bay another rising trout was located, but the violence of the wind made it necessary to cast too tight a line in order to drop the fly in the glass edge, with the result that a drag began to develop immediately, putting the trout down. A few yards higher a clump of trees made a sort of buffer of air, and the conditions were a bit easier. Yet, though the sun came out and showed the Red Quill gliding down the glass edge, the rise of the next trout was such a delicately neat movement that the angler was once again almost taken unawares. Yet this time he fastened, and his first fish of the day, after a dumbfounded second's pause, forged upstream with a rush, tearing line from the protesting reel. He was not, however, allowed to reach his holt among the weeds, but was turned, and netted out thirty yards or so downstream, after a strenuous resistance. The hook was on the extreme edge of his upper lip, but, fortunately, had taken a beautifully firm hold. The spring-balance recorded one pound fifteen ounces—rather a disappointment, for his hogback and splendour of general condition suggested that he might, though a short sixteen inches, have topped two pounds.

A moment sufficed to knot on a fresh fly, and the very first cast into the glass edge, to a glide where a dimple betrayed a trout, produced another rise; and again the offer was accepted, and an excellent fight put up. When eventually netted out, the fish proved to be one pound nine ounces, and even handsomer and finer in condition than number one. He was hooked exactly in the same way. There was one more rise spotted, the fish risen, touched, and seen in the clearness of the glass edge to flash some yards upstream under the far bank. Then the sun went in for a spell, and all was over for the day. The other angler had a brace—two pounds ten ounces and one pound odd—caught in the same way by floating the Red Quill in the glass edge.

This was one of those rare days when the dry fly can be fished into the bays under the opposite bank.

OF THE CROSS-COUNTRY CAST.

If questioned on their favourite mode of approaching a trout, it is probable that nineteen out of every twenty chalk-stream anglers, if not a larger proportion, would plump for the right bank with the rod held over the water. It is doubtless the easiest method. It has various advantages not difficult to enumerate, but it may be gravely doubted whether it is the most effective from the point of view of catching trout. Later under the caption ("The Bank of Vantage") it is shown—with what success the reader must judge—that in most states of the wind the left bank has, contrary to general opinion (other things, of course, being equal), decided advantages over the right.

Apart from states of the wind, it must be apparent that, where the horizontal cast is used, and often where the cast is not strictly horizontal, the left bank has the advantage over the right that the rod and line are less displayed, and far less likely to alarm a wary fish under the angler's own bank than a rod held more or less over the stream; and, naturally, it is only to a fish under the angler's own bank that the cross-country cast is made.

Secondly, there is the advantage that little of the line—possibly not all of the gut, even—strikes the water. It is enough if the drag and the recovery occur far enough below the fish not to disturb him; but if the fly be the right pattern the drag is a matter of no consequence, as the cross-country cast comes so lightly, so naturally, and with such concealment of its perils from the trout, that as often as not he takes the fly at the first offer.

Of course, the vegetation on the bank may be such as to render it almost impossible to deliver this cast without being hung up, but the angler should not be too ready to assume that this is so. It is wonderful how, with care, a light hand and a little patience, the line may be recovered, and what risks may be taken with comparative impunity. It is often astonishing to see how anglers who pay largely for their fishing rights, own costly rods, reels, and lines, and make long train journeys for their fishing, will decline to tackle trout in difficult-positions, because it involves the possible loss of a cast or a fly—perhaps 1s. $2\frac{1}{2}$d.* all told—with the odds long in favour of the loss being no more than a fly, and perhaps a point. I am ever for the adventure. The certain smash does not always come off.

But after the meadows are cut, and when the sedges are low, it is often excellent sport to beat slowly up on either bank, left or right, keeping in either case well inland—especially so on the right bank—and flicking a grass moth or a small sedge dry into every little eddy and bay, and on to every likely spot under the bank, with never more than three feet—or four feet at the outside—of gut on the water (often not more than eighteen inches or a foot). Of course, a rod which will cast a short line accurately is indispensable. The fly lights like thistledown. On such days, if you work orthodoxly up your right bank, casting a longish line upstream, and covering the water with it, you shall not hook one fish for three which you shall take with the cross-country cast. Then, to recover it, you must either draw it slowly over the edge where the danger lies, or you must flick the line up so as to belly vertically away from you, and pick the gut and fly cleanly off the water or the herbage. And if occasionally you are hung up, what does it matter? If it be of service, the angler is not denied such relief as the golfer freely avails himself of when the deadly bunker has him for its own.

* Pre-war prices.

MAINLY TACTICAL

WHAT TUSSOCKS ARE FOR.

This is not a riddle. It is a speculation which many anglers have probably indulged in. Some have considered them a providential arrangement for the protection of the business of the dealer in flies and tackle, and verily they have their reasons. At one time I was of that fold, but of late years I have had glimpses of the other side of the shield, and I am beginning to realize that while tussocks may be put along river-sides as a trial of the patience of some, yet for others they are a means of providing an occasional trout, and generally a good one, on days when disappointment is king. They are placed, in other words, for the trout to stand on the upstream side and the angler on the downstream side, the latter substantially concealed from the former. It is equally true that the former is also concealed from the latter; but this is of little consequence if, as is commonly the case, the screen is not dense enough to hide the ring from the angler when the trout takes his fly.

But it may be said, "What is the use of the concealment if the inevitable result of casting over the tussock is to get hung up in it?" Well, it is not the inevitable result. There are two ways of tackling a tussock. One implies the use of a short rod, or at least a rod capable of an accurate short cast. It will not do to dib. At the first glimpse of the rod-top over the tussock off goes your trout. No; the fly must be cast, and cast so near the tussock that it drifts down to the fish just above the tussock before it is necessary to pick it up for the next cast with a forward flick. The other method is to cast over the river side of the drooping sedges of the tussock from such a distance that only the gut and a foot or two of the casting line go on to the water above the tussock, and to let the belly of the line dip in the water between you and the tussock. Then, if the fly be not taken, the angler shall see his line coming back smoothly and at the pace of the stream over the tussock, and finally the fly shall be lifted off the surface with no disturbance, and be drawn by the current softly over the tussock, and drop on the surface on his own side, free for the next attempt.

Obviously, this latter cast is not well suited to the left bank unless the angler fish left-handed, and, then, it is not suited to the right bank, unless he be ambidextrous. *Ergo*, the rod which casts a short line with delicacy and accuracy is a desideratum for this business, as for many others. A heavy rod will seldom be found to do it. When you have hooked your fish, he may be depended on to carry your line at once free of the tussock. I have never had an instance to the contrary, and I have rather an affection for the tussock cast.

OF THE ALLEGED MARCH BROWN.

Everyone who reads much angling literature must have come across ingenuous arguments on the wonderful usefulness of the March Brown even on waters, such as the chalk streams, where the natural is not found. It is so. I have found it so myself. One 6th of April some years back I reached the Wey, to find that the Grannom was well on a good week in advance of time, and that I had one imitation, and one only, in my box. To improve upon the humour of the situation, I allowed—nay, I forced—the first trout to whom I presented it to keep it. But was I downhearted? No! I had some small floating March Browns, which, with the whisks pinched off, made quite satisfactory Grannoms and saved the situation. On other occasions I have used Grannom and March Brown indifferently to represent the grass-moths with which the meadows and banks were teeming, and they each did the job excellently and were most attractive. I have also used the March Brown as a Brown Silver Horns, and to simulate other sedges, and there is no doubt that it is an excellent fly, and, as generally tied, quite a poor imitation of the natural March Brown, and quite a passable imitation of almost anything else.

GENERAL FLIES AND FANCY FLIES.

The alleged March Brown may be called a "general fly"—*i.e.*, it is a more or less satisfactory imitation, not merely of one, but of many flies. In the same way the Red Quill is a general fly, covering not only a series of red spinners, but also probably the whirling blue dun. Tup's Indispensable used as a floater is an excellent rendering of many red spinners. The sunk variety is an efficient rendering of many nymphs. No. 1 Whitchurch is, I see, included by Mr. F. M. Halford among fancy flies; but I should venture to class it as "general," being an effective presentment of the yellow dun series of flies. Greenwell's Glory, again, is a general fly, and with its starling-winged variants it represents a series of olives, from the blue-winged olive to the iron blue (male).

It is hard to say what precisely are fancy flies, unless one defines them as flies which are not known to represent definitely any insect or class of insects. Whether Wickham's Fancy to the eye of a trout looks the gorgeous golden thing which it does to mankind it is hard to say. I have floated one on water over a mirror, and the reflected image did not look golden at all, but a pale, dim green, much like the colour seen through gold beaten so thin that it is almost transparent. The Pink Wickham may seem to the trout to be a sedge with a greenish body. The Red Tag *may* have its living prototype. The Soldier Palmer is supposed to represent the soldier beetle. But in most of these cases it is impossible to say what the artificial represents, or may represent, in life, and its attraction is apt to be that of something bright and garish which appeals to curiosity or tyranny in the trout, rather than to appetite. Indeed, why a trout should take any artificial fly is a puzzle to me. The very best are not really very like the real thing. One thing is clear: It is not form which appeals to the trout, but colour and size.

I know a skilful angler who, when he ties on a new split-winged floater, rumples and breaks up the fibre of its wings with his fingers before using it. This he does for the excellent reason that it pays. His theory is that it lets the light through; but form is entirely sacrificed.

It is a curious fact that, though the Test and Itchen are "by ordinar'" clear, yet double-dressed floaters can be successfully used on them, which would do little or nothing on other streams, of which the Wandle occurs to me as an example.* If I had a day on the Wandle, I should take care to provide myself with single-winged patterns. Can it be that the clearness of the Test and Itchen is such that the fly looks distinct enough by reflected light, while transmitted light is necessary to render the fly noticeable on such streams as the Wandle? In any case, when visiting a strange river, the angler should see if the fish will or will not stand double-dressed floaters, if he has a fancy for that build of fly.

* The Derbyshire Wye is another example.

CHAPTER IX

CONSIDERATIONS, MORAL, TACTICAL, PSYCHOLOGICAL, AND INCIDENTAL

OF FAITH.

AMONG the many uncertainties which attend the sport of fly-fishing, there is one thing that may be laid down as certain, and that is that no consistent measure of success attends a lure, whether wet, dry, or semi-submerged, in which the angler has not faith; and it may be shrewdly suspected that much of the ill-success which has attended the use of the wet fly upon chalk streams in the past is due to lack of confidence on the part of the angler. It has been laid down so positively by the high-priests of the dry fly that the wet fly has no chance compared with it—at any rate, on smooth water—and it has been so freely stated that crack wet-fly anglers come down to the chalk streams confident in their powers to make an exhibition of chalk-stream fish, only to retire defeated and converted, that it is little wonder that the chalk-stream angler who tries the wet fly does it half-heartedly; and it is probable that the North-Country man coming to practise his art upon South-Country streams, and accustomed to catch his trout in considerable numbers, soon becomes disheartened by failure to do the like on rivers where two or three brace is a good bag. Probably he casts a much shorter line than is advisable on chalk streams, and so scares off or puts down his fish; and discouragement and the sceptical attitude of his South-Country hosts and their keepers knock him off his game before he has had time to adjust himself to the (to him) novel conditions.

Fishing a chalk stream with a wet fly is not quite like fishing a mountain stream or North-Country river, and it is not a game to be learnt in an hour or a day. But if the angler will fix his mind firmly on the fact that the wet fly was for centuries the only method in use on chalk streams, and that it brought excellent baskets to good anglers in the past, he may set to work with confidence that in the right conditions the wet fly will kill, and kill well, at this day, and he may set himself with equal confidence to find out for himself how it is done. And let him not be disturbed by the fact that there are days or hours when it has not a chance against the dry fly; for there are days and hours when the dry fly has not a chance against it, and there are other occasions when the trout will take either with approximately equal freedom.

Simultaneously with my own experiments recorded in this volume, Mr. F. M. Halford was engaged in establishing and proving his latest series of patterns, in which he endeavours to approximate more closely than ever before to the coloration and attitude of the natural insects, especially in his series of spinners. In an article over the signature "Detached Badger," which appeared in the *Field* of October 22, 1904, Mr. Halford was at some pains to prove that these spinners must be taken floating; but the feature of these patterns is that they do not, like the old patterns, sit cocked upon the surface, lifted half-hackle-high above it, but, being sparsely dressed, lie low on the water, practically flush with the surface, and thus achieve a closer approximation to the spent natural insect than did the old patterns. This, as much as the more exact coloration, may account for the success of these patterns. And, after all, a fly that is flush with the water is perilously close to the edge of wet. Tup's Indispensable fished as a spinner in the evening rise will often kill better semi-submerged and flush with the surface than thoroughly dried and oiled. It usually serves me well, and I have accordingly scarcely tried Mr. F. M. Halford's new patterns, but when I have done so it has been wet that they have been taken, and not dry.

CONSIDERATIONS MORAL, TACTICAL, PYSCHOLOGICAL

I mentioned a few pages back that another Itchen angler once fished the whole of a season—it may have been two—with the Red Quill in various shades and sizes, and with differences introduced by the presence or omission of tinsel tags, and he achieved a success with that one pattern or type quite as great as he enjoyed when he allowed himself the full range of the "hundred best" and some others.

Clearly, he and "Detached Badger" have had faith—the faith which, if it does not move mountains, will at least move trout. And the angler who takes his courage in both hands and experiments boldly with the wet fly fished upstream to his trout, or into the place where his trout should be, will find his faith, as mine has been, not without its reward.

OF THE BANK OF VANTAGE.

In looking back on a day's fly-fishing, one can realize how much has depended upon the correct selection of the bank to fish from, and an examination of some of the more important of the general considerations governing choice may not be amiss. Special conditions, such as height of banks, the trees and bushes thereon, and the accessibility of the water therefrom, may force upon us deviations from what our judgment would otherwise dictate, and it is impossible to dogmatize about these. There are also cases where the winding character of the stream presents such a constant variety of conditions that it is impossible to say that at the moment of selection one bank is more worthy of choice than the other. But, subject to such special conditions, there are a few general principles which it is well to bear in mind in considering from which side we shall direct our attack.

The first of these is to avoid such a position as will throw the shadow of angler or rod over the fish. This is an obvious consideration, and one that is easy of application. But it does not necessarily follow that, because the sun will throw one's shadow—even a long or formidable shadow—on to the stream from, say, the right bank, one must necessarily adopt the other. It may be that the shadow will be straight across or even behind the angler, or, at any rate, in such a position as, for instance, not to interfere with his casting upstream, or upstream and across, and the river bottom may not be so bare that the fall of his shadow will send the trout scurrying upstream to disturb and put down the feeding fish above. In narrow streams, however, the effect of shadow in bolting fish upstream is necessarily far more pronounced than in streams of moderate width—say twelve to twenty yards. In like manner, the narrow stream should not, if possible, even with a favouring upstream breeze, be fished from the right bank, which necessitates holding the rod and waving line and fly over the water, or one may see one's hopes laid low for half an hour or more, and a good stretch spoiled by the bolting of fish which, approached from the other bank by a more or less "cross-country" cast, with the rod held low to the right, might have been brought to basket or turned downstream.

Probably, however, the most generally governing consideration is the direction of the wind in relation to the general trend of the stream. Perhaps the majority of fly-fishermen, if asked to choose a bank with an upstream or downstream wind, would choose the right without hesitation. But there may be a good deal to be said for the other side, apart even from the sun and the narrowness of the stream. For instance, with an upstream wind and a fairly wide river, especially if it be swift, the angler on the right bank is practically confined to his own bank and midstream fishing. If he casts for the opposite bank, he finds it extremely difficult to be accurate, and a drag which inevitably puts the fish down is almost certain to be set up. On the left bank, however, not only can he approach the left bankers more closely than he dare approach the right bankers when fishing on the right bank, not only can he tackle the mid-stream fish equally well, but he can cut under and against the wind and get across to the opposite bank far more accurately from the left bank than from the right, where the wind follows his hand.

Take next the case of a downstream wind. Here the angler will want to consider what he has to do. Does he wish to fish his own bank or the opposite bank, or both? Casting from the right bank, he can cut under the wind and get his fly over to the opposite bank far better than he could from the left; but is it worth doing? If he can float his fly for a reasonable distance without drag, it may well be; but if the current be so strong as to set up an almost immediate drag, he may be practically confined to his own bank. So he would be on the left side; but whereas casting from the right bank he would be apt to find the point of his gut cast forced outwards and downwards by the wind, and be constantly landing his line on the sedges or bank, when casting from the other side his line would fall upon the water, and the gut-point and fly be driven inwards so as to search the water quite close under the bank, just like a natural fly. Moreover, it would not be driven so far inward as it would be driven outward when cast from the opposite side, for in dropping over the bank-edge the fly and gut-point would enter, before the force of the cast is spent, into that little cushion of calm to be found just under the bank, and would generally straighten out in a manner to command admiration both from men and trout.

Take next the case of an upstream wind slightly across from the right bank to the left. Here it is even more difficult for an angler on the right bank to fish his own bank than for an angler on the left bank, while he has more command in cutting across to the far side from the left bank than from the right. If, on the other hand, the wind be upstream and off the left bank, by standing back a bit and using a short cross-country cast, the angler may get his fly very neatly over most of the fish under his own bank, and can cut across more easily than he could from the right bank.

Take, again, the case of a wind downstream and across from the right bank to the left. Here again the angler on the left bank is in the superior position for negotiating his own bank, casting almost straight into the wind, and letting fly and point be deflected under his own bank. On the right bank the angler would be apt to have his fly flung out towards midstream, and the short cross-country cast would be apt to miscarry. On the other hand, if the wind be downstream and across from the left bank, the advantage lies slightly with the right bank, but it is nothing like so marked (assuming, as we have been doing from the first, that the angler is right-handed) as in the converse case.

On the whole, therefore, it will be seen that, contrary to the generally received opinion, unless the wind be fairly direct upstream or (for fishing the opposite bank) down, the left bank is almost invariably the bank of vantage.

OF COURAGE AND THE JEOPARDIZING OF TUPPENCE HA'PENNY.

That, my friends, is almost the extreme price of a trout-fly. Some cost less.* Yet how often shall you see an angler whose equipment for the taking of trout has run into pounds, and whose railway fare and reckoning at his inn are substantial items of expenditure upon the same object, throw away most sporting occasions for the attainment of his end because, forsooth, he is sure to be hung up or weeded or smashed or something equally delightful—and bang would go tuppence ha'penny! I have no patience with this sort of thing. The more hopeless the prospect of getting out a trout from an impossible place, the more determined I am to try for him. *De l'audace, encore de l'audace—toujours de l'audace!* In May, 1909, just before the May-fly began, I was by the river-side, when I heard a loud smacking sound, and, peering through a willow-bush, I saw a fine trout

*Alas! this is no longer. But the moral is the same.

cruising on an eddy and sucking down flies with hearty enjoyment. If I cast over him from behind the bush, I should have to play him on a six-ounce rod with x x x gut between a thornbush which I could touch with my right hand and a willow I could touch with my left. There were snags above and snags below. Did I hesitate? Only long enough to tie on a new Crosbie Alder, then long enough for him to reach the top of his beat, and then I dropped the fly behind him just before he turned. He was the satisfactory side of four pounds, and I got his successor next day out of the same place—three pounds six ounces. A beautiful brace! Luck! Of course it was luck, but I shouldn't have had it if I hadn't taken risks.

There was a Kennet trout under a willow in May-fly time. A weed-piled snag in the stream just below the droop of the willow made it impossible to get a fly over him by casting above the willow and floating down. There was just one possible way—to make a slanting downward cut which might bring the fly down between branches in a sort of dip in the tree, and drop it on the fish's nose. I left two flies in the tree, but I did the trick and got the fish. He was only two pounds six ounces, but I thought he was bigger. Still——

Then there was a fish which lay just above a hatch-hole through which water ran into the meadows. The inevitable thing for him to do when hooked was to bolt down the hatch-hole. But somehow he didn't, and I got him. There was a pound-and-a-half trout taking tiny pale duns on the edge of a small pile of weeds collected against a broken bough of a tree, into which he was sure to bolt when hooked. But somehow he didn't, and he was steered to the landing-net with a No. 000 dun on gossamer gut attached to his nose. Then there was that trout which I got over a barbed wire crossing the stream eight or ten yards away.

There are countless such instances—I tell of some more under the head of "Impossible Places"—but there is one thing that may safely be deposed to, and that is, that there is no place so desperate that, with luck and management, you may not get a well-hooked trout out of it.

OF IMPOSSIBLE PLACES.

The habit of a lightly hooked trout, of floundering on the surface, is too well known to need enlarging on. Sometimes his antics will be varied by leaps into the air. But is the tendency of a hard-held fish to go to weed or snag equally well realized? Yet from a consideration of these two established tendencies may not a highly unorthodox method of extricating a good fish from the impossible position be evolved? What is the theory? This: Let him think he is lightly hooked.

It was on the banks of the Itchen that the first glimmerings of the idea suggested themselves. A novice with the dry fly was walking disconsolate up the stream, bemoaning himself that he could not find a rising fish. Coming up with a brother angler just about to settle down to a rising trout in some quick water, he was invited to cast over it. The fly covered the right spot, and brought up his troutship, who fastened, and, turning at once, bolted at express speed down-stream. The novice, unaccustomed to anything more formidable than Devonshire brook trout, disregarded his companion's advice, "Run, man, run downstream for all you're worth!" and backed, open-mouthed, slowly upstream, letting out line as freely as the reel (a checkless one) would let it go. So long as the line put no check upon him the trout ploughed downstream close to the surface, but the moment the reel was empty and he felt the check he was deep in a weed-bed. He stayed there till the angler had reeled up and put on another fly. *The checked fish goes to weed.* That was the first lesson.

The second was in this wise: On a September morning a good many years back, a brace of trout were rising, a yard or so apart, above a tree which overhung the same water on the side where the angler stood knee-deep in a swampy reed-bed. It was possible to reach them if, holding by his left hand to a bough, and resting one foot on a root while dangling the other in the water, he hung over the river at an angle of forty-five degrees, and threw his line underhand up the stream. But how if he hooked his fish? There was a bank of weeds, dense and long, a yard or two above. Well, he must chance it. The likelihood of losing the fish seemed overwhelming, the chance of killing him slight; for the position was so awkward that, in order to get back to terra firma, there was nothing for it but to tuck the rod under the arm and trust to chance while recovering equilibrium and a footing. Yet the angler got both these fish. Situated as he was he could put no pressure on them; he could not even keep the line taut. But each of the fish when hooked came floundering and splattering unresistingly downstream, trying to throw out the stinging insect that adhered to his jaw. By the time the angler was prepared to deal with him the fish was in open water and was easily played. Result, a brace of one and a quarter pounders and the second lesson. *The unchecked fish flounders on the surface.*

What these two lessons have been worth to the angler it would be tedious to relate, but one or two instances may illustrate. There was that fish—one and three-quarter pounds he proved—rising on the far side of a dense bank of weeds in a channel two feet wide. He had to be approached with reverence on one's face, and from twenty feet out in the meadow. He took the Pink Wickham at the first time of asking, and the angler, having fastened, dropped his rod-point instantly. The fish with a startled plunge rushed up the channel and out into the open water, and began to flounder. Before he knew where he was the angler turned him, brought him down the right side of the dangerous weed-bank, and duly netted him out.

Then, again, there was that black fish between two pollard willows on the Darenth. He was rising eighteen inches out from the bank. The willows were two yards apart, and their roots formed a mass of snags below him, while just downstream of them was a plank bridge a foot above the river. Here again it was a case of kneeling far out in the meadow and dropping the Yellow Dun exactly over the nose of the fish. He came with the most confiding simplicity. Had he been checked he would have been in the snags before one could say "Knife," but the angler, mindful of his lesson, held him not. So it befell that he rushed out into midstream and leapt four several times, much as does a pricked fish that is not hooked at all. But ere he could do more the angler was on terms with him, and held him out from the bank, up from the bottom, and away from the plank bridge, till the landing-net received his one pound six ounces.

Finally, let the tale be told of a trout of the Kennet that had his holt in a corner of a little bay, whence a willow-bush had fallen into the river, leaving on the bank side a tangle of broken roots, in the river to the right, some three yards off, the half-submerged willow, while above and below were heavy patches of long swaying weed. It was an ideal place for a trout to feed in—and to break away. The water came into the bay in a little defined channel between weeds, and in this, a foot below the entry, a sizeable neb was showing at intervals. A small Green Champion May dropped exactly in the channel, and trotted down the prescribed distance and disappeared. Again the tactics of the loosened line, again the hooked fish rushed out from his almost impregnable holt into the open, and was presently netted out by the triumphant angler—a handsome and, he thinks, a not ill-deserved three pounds ten ounces. A week later the same tactics produced another fish of two pounds eleven ounces from the same hole.

OF THE USE OF THE LANDING NET.

There is a common superstition among anglers that the primary use of a landing-net is to land fish. Let us rather say that the use of a landing-net, rightly understood, is to assist in the capture of fish. Not to catch fish, for the catching of fish in the landing-net is mere poacher's work, but to aid in the catching.

CONSIDERATIONS MORAL, TACTICAL, PYSCHOLOGICAL

Some anglers tell you you must never show your net to a fish until ready for netting. But why not, if it will help you to kill him? There are many more or less desperate cases where the net may be of the profoundest service long before it is called to operate at the final ceremony of dipping out. I will give one or two examples in an ascending scale of complexity.

Firstly, a new use for the handle. Under the left bank of a South-Country chalk stream a trout is taking every dun that goes down alongside the cluster of cut weed under which he shelters. The angler's Gold-ribbed Hare's Ear lighting delicately a foot above, with the gut resting on the weed, is accepted and carried straight down into the weed-bed below. The angler reels up tight over the fish, but fails to move him. Ah, there is the long-handled landing-net! A few judiciously-placed prods with the butt bring him plunging stupidly out, and he is bustled down into open water and promptly dipped out with the other end.

Secondly, the use of the mesh. Scene: A hooked fish racing downstream towards a dense weed-bed on the angler's side. The angler offers the net, and the fish sheers off into midstream, and is towed past the dangerous obstruction. Very simple examples these.

The third and next is more complex. Scene: A hatch-hole which lets water from the same stream into a carrier in the water-meadows. Camp-sheathing on both sides of the hatch, supported by three successive crossbars from four feet to eight feet long as the sides diverge. Under the middle bar lies a good trout, very evidently feeding. Problem, how to get him. It is impossible to cast underneath the crossbars. One can only cast over them, and trust to luck and judgment to get the fish out if one hooks him. If he runs downstream the line is doubled over the crossbar and a break is assured. But how is he to be prevented? The angler knows that under the apron of the hatch there is a big hole, and he sets to work with confidence. The fly is dropped from below, just over the third or shortest bar. The drag of the oiled silk line brings it back till it passes over the third bar, and drops softly on the water with a foot or two to float before it can drag. Presently it is taken, and the hooked fish has turned to bolt down the carrier. But there the angler is ready. Landing-net in hand, he gesticulates wildly at the advancing fish, which bolts upstream again and buries itself in the hole under the apron. Softly the rod is passed under the second and lowest crossbars, then the point is brought down to the water's edge, and with a steady strain and a jarring tap on the butt of the rod the trout is brought down out of his fastness and killed in due course.

Lastly, another example of a similar method. Imagine a strong stream some three yards wide and one hundred yards or so long, running down from a similar hatch to a big cross-dyke reaching out on both sides. The angler is on the right bank, and the current turns to the left on reaching the dyke. The water for the latter half of the carrier is too deep for wading. In the broad gravel shallow at the tail of the patch a big two-pounder is lying. The angler has already been run by a much smaller fish down to the verge of the carrier, where the stream turns off, and only netted his trout just in time. For various reasons the other bank is unsuitable to fish from. To begin with, the big trout is not accessible from that side. Even from the left bank it is difficult to cast over him, but presently our artist with the landing-net gives the appropriate response to the dimpling rise with which he takes the Ginger Quill, and a good sound working connection is established. For a moment the angler does not put a pull on him, and he moves out into the strong water, shaking his head to get rid of that objectionable insect that has fastened in his palate. The angler rapidly winds in line, and begins to hold him firmly. His aim is to keep him tiring himself in the strong water—not to drive him up under the apron (it is unnecessary to run that risk now), but to keep him from running down. The stream is narrow enough to enable the angler, by dipping his rod-point to right or left, to turn the fish from every upward rush to such a holt, but

CONSIDERATIONS MORAL, TACTICAL, PYSCHOLOGICAL

in a few moments comes the downward rush. Now for the landing-net. In an instant the fish has turned and is back facing the strong water, and engaged in fighting to get up into the shelter of the hatch. But again and again he is turned and brought down to the edge of the gravel shelf where the stream is strongest, when a hint from the landing-net sends him up again straining with all his force against both stream and line. Presently, tiring of the game, and failing in his efforts to rub out the hook against the camp-sheathing, he turns and bolts downstream with such suddenness as to evade the threatening net, and is gone forty yards before the angler is level with him. Then again a threat of the net turns him, and he makes a dash for a weed-bed some ten yards or so above. From this he has to be turned down, and his downward rush stopped with the net as before. From this point the fight resolves itself into a series of downstream rushes, alternating with much briefer trips upstream, terminated by the necessity in each case for pulling the trout down out of the weed-bed he is bolting for. At last, at the very bottom of the straight, on the edge of the dyke, the fish, not yet half beaten, has to be dragged willy-nilly into the landing-net, or else he must escape down the dyke which streams away on the far side.

Finally, and in conclusion, one more example. The *locus in quo* is a piece of fast water some eight or ten yards long, a sort of tumbling-bay, from which the water escapes at racing pace through a culvert twelve or fourteen feet long, which passes under a farm road, thence along some two hundred yards of narrow weedy carrier to an irrigation hatch. In the tumbling-bay are three or four fine fish, one of them something over two pounds. All are feeding on something under water, probably nymphs. A dry fly would drag at once. A double-hooked Greenwell's Glory, as used on North-Country rivers, might do the trick. But the hooked fish will to a certainty bolt down the culvert, and then it will be a case of smash at once, or weeding with a long line, and the impossible task of bringing the fish up the racing stream into the tumbling-bay again, or of passing the ten-foot rod through a twelve-foot culvert. Happy thought! there on the bank is a plank that has been floated down the stream above, there is some string, and there is the watcher to lend a hand. He receives the landing-net, and goes below some fifteen yards or so. Presently the fly drops well soaked on the water, and swings over the best of the trout, which the next minute has raced down and through the culvert, tearing out line until—yes, until the menacing net in the hands of the watcher sends him securely to weed. Now for the plank. A minute serves to tie on the rod and to send the plank floating down through the culvert. The watcher is ready on the other side with the landing-net, and draws the plank to the side. The rod is released, and soon the angler stands over the fish with a short line. Now for the net again. A few well-directed prods with the butt brings up the fish, who bolts for the culvert. But the net is before him on the far side, and he gets back into the tumbling-bay. Guiding the line with the butt, a pull is got on him which soon brings him down again below the culvert. The only remaining dangers are the weeds and the hatch-hole at the far end. From this last the net is again ready to keep him, and the great battle ends as every such battle should.

OF THE WEEDING TROUT.

It has been shown how it was frequently possible to extract a big trout from an apparently impossible fastness by a tactical trick. Every angler knows that a trout who is, or conceives himself to be, lightly hooked will thrash about upon the surface in his effort to dislodge the fly, very often with success, though not always; for occasionally the hook will have a small but sufficient hold in some inaccessible place, such as the corner of the jaw, and all is well with the angler. It is by playing upon this idiosyncrasy and slackening on a fish immediately after it is hooked that the trout may frequently be induced to run from an impenc-

CONSIDERATIONS MORAL, TACTICAL, PYSCHOLOGICAL

trable holt into the open in order to kick himself free from the surface. The same idiosyncrasy may be worked upon with a weeding fish, with gratifying results. If the angler hooks a fish which turns and bolts downstream below him, he will note that the fish will not go to weed until he is held. The moment he is held he will whip into the first available weed-bed. That is the first step in our argument. The next is this: The harder he is held the more frightened he becomes, and the deeper and the more desperately he will burrow in the weeds.

But one day it occurred to me to try upon the trout that has got to weed the tactics of inducing him to believe himself lightly hooked. To let him go altogether for a time till he recovered his nerve and came out was an old and often unsuccessful device. To hand-line him was to put a much harder pull upon him than could be put on with a rod, and though it sometimes worked, it was by no means always successful. For the new method, therefore, it was necessary to maintain a light pull upon the fish, but so light that the rod-top gave to every movement, leaving the fish almost as free as if he were loose, but with just the difference that there was enough strain to keep him beating, and enough to provide a fulcrum for him to beat from. The experiment was brilliantly successful. On the first occasion on which it was tried, three trout (all over two pounds) were hooked in a weedy portion of the Itchen upon the lightest tackle and a delicate rod. Each went to weed. The angler held his hand high (for the rod was but nine feet), and kept the very lightest strain, with the result that the fish began to beat among the weeds as he would on the surface, and in a few moments had lashed the weeds aside and kicked himself free of them, and was on top. Once there he was resolutely hauled downstream and bustled into the net. This method has been worth many a good fish since that day; indeed, given a fairly soundly hooked fish, there have been no failures. Of course, nothing will save a fish so lightly hooked that the first touch of weed or obstruction releases him. In applying this method, the light rod, which has come to be so common, has an advantage over the big, heavy, and clumsy weapon so frequently in the hands of dry-fly men in the recent past. This is indeed a notable instance of the superiority of the *suaviter in modo* over the *fortiter in re*.

OF THE LIGHT ROD ON CHALK STREAMS.

In the catalog (I quote the word in the American spelling) of the house of William Mills and Son of New York there is a portrait of Mr. Humphrey Priddis (whose signature "Dabchick" at the foot of Itchen reports is familiar to all readers of the *Field*) holding up a two and one-eighth pound trout which he had just killed on a two and one-eighth ounce Leonard rod, the property of young Mr. Mills, a son of that house. I was down on the Itchen the afternoon on which that feat was done. I saw the rod, the fish, and the captor, and the place was pointed out to me. The water was full of dense masses of waving weeds, and in accomplishing the capture of such a fish—a large one for the water—on such a rod there is no doubt that the angler executed a feat of which he had every right to be proud. He declared himself amazed at the power of the rod, and that he could throw three-and-twenty yards with it.

Young Mr. Mills was fishing with a nine-foot rod weighing five ounces, a delightful tool capable of casting a heavy tapered Halford line with wonderful command. I had the privilege of trying it, and I promptly acquired its duplicate,* in addition to the ten-footer of the same make which I already possessed and had used the previous season.

I am not going to reargue here the long controversy of light rod *versus* the old-style ounce-to-the-foot weapon. The light rod has won its place, and has come to stay. Those who have tried it fairly are convinced that it will answer all necessary calls for

---

* This rod, after eighteen years' hard wear, is still my favourite.

CONSIDERATIONS MORAL, TACTICAL, PYSCHOLOGICAL

casting, that it is fully equal to butting and killing large trout, and that it adds a daintiness to the art of fly-fishing which the old-time anglers of the heavy rod were hardly conscious it lacked. But I do want to press three points in its favour beyond those enumerated: (1) It casts a delightful *short* line, and I confess to fishing consistently with the shortest line I dare use, often with most of that in the country; (2) it can be fished steadily all day, wet or dry, without tiring the hand—what a change from those terrible wrist-breaking, hand-paralyzing, blister-producing flails of the eighties and nineties! and (3) it enables one to play light with unequalled sensitiveness. When I was a boy at Winchester, old John Hammond had the length commonly known nowadays as Chalkley's, and I well remember the rods which old John used to turn out for fishing the Itchen. They were soft and floppy to an extent which would nowadays lead to their immediate rejection; but I have seen the maker with one of them steer a good fish, hooked under the opposite bank, by sheer handling, over dense weed, into the waiting landing-net. And remembering this, and remembering how a fish which goes to weed can, if lightly handled from the first, be forced, by play on his idiosyncrasy, to beat himself free and up to the surface, I am inclined to think that the modern angler is far too much inclined to use force in handling a hooked fish, and that a rod which achieves—as the light split canes of the highest class do—a combination of steely quickness and casting power with something of the sensitive delicacy of the wood rods of old John Hammond is the equipment to have in a tussle with a big fish on fine tackle.

To kill a brace of trout one of over four pounds and the other three pounds six ounces on x x x gut in deep weedy and snag-infested water between two bushes which I could touch with either hand, and which prevented movement up or down stream, is a feat which I am sure my old-time heavy rods could have done no better than did my six-ounce ten-footer in 1909. Force was no good in such a place, and force was never used until each trout had been sufficiently bewildered and fatigued by beating in vain against the nothing which restrained him to be kept more or less under the rod's point till ready for the net.

OF WET-FLY CASTING.

The use of rods which carry a heavy reel line is so general on chalk streams that probably the easy drying of the fly and cast is taken as a matter of course, and it is little recognized how much is due to the weight of the line driving the fly rapidly through the air. If the angler were devoting himself to wet-fly fishing on a rough river, he would avoid such a casting line, and if he means to fish a chalk stream wet-fly only, he will do the same. But he would need to be able to propel his fly and line upstream against the wind, and to cast a fairly long line not infrequently, so that a line with more weight in it than would be required for a rough river would be essential on a chalk stream. But if, as is the wiser course, the angler proposes to fish either wet or dry, as occasion demands, his equipment must be still more of a compromise. He must use a rod which will carry a line that will dry the fly with sufficient speed, but preferably not a line of the heaviest class; and he must trust to the make of his flies, and to the soaking they get through trailing in the water before the cast, to get them to go under on lighting. The knack can be acquired without difficulty, but if the dry-fly habit has become inveterate he will need to be continually watching himself when he desires to fish wet.

The line should be flicked as little as possible, and the angler should try (generally speaking, but not always—see chapter on Nerves) to float the gut while letting the fly go under. Then he secures the double advantage of not lining his trout and of getting an indication from the movement of the gut should the fly be taken without his otherwise detecting it. The fly, being once delivered, may be allowed to come down with the stream precisely like a dry fly except for its being under water; but it can be recovered sooner and with less disturbance of the surface, because the fly is drawn under and not along the top of the water. The withdrawal should, however, be as gentle as possible, in order to retain as much moisture as can be in the fly to sink it at the next cast. If there be enough wind to raise waves, or even a strong ruffle, this is of less consequence, as the make of the fly should be such that it can only float, if at all, while quite dry on perfectly smooth water. It is in general no use to put up the ordinary dry flies to fish wet.

CHAPTER X

FRANKLY IRRELEVANT

A DRY-FLY MEMORY.

In the Test Valley a good many years ago the coarse herbage lay drying in the water-meadows in the heavy swathes in which it had fallen to the scythe, but all along the boggy edges of the streams and carriers a tall screen had ben left standing shoulder-high, concealing the angler from the rising fish, but compelling him, unfortunately, to stand and to fish overhand instead of keeping low and switching a horizontal line to his quarry. During the afternoon a chilly wind from the north-west had supervened upon the blazing heat that for a week past had conjured such alluring visions of the evening rise to end each July day. The sky was overcast, and a troubled sun watched sulkily from the far side of the valley, through dun rifts in the clouds, the approach of two rods to the riverside. It was almost too early to begin. Scarce a fly was in the air, and only one sign of any promise gave any hint of possible success—the horses in the meadow opposite, driven to madness by the Hampshire flies, were charging and careering wildly about their pasture, heels half the time in air.

Just a cast above the bottom boundary was a run which promised a moving fish when the trout began to move, and half an hour's wait in these exquisite meadows was time well spent, if only in observing the splendid profusion of life in this wonderful valley. The tender bloom of the meadowsweet was at its most perfect, great wild purple orchids put up among the boggy tussocks, while the lush richness of the water-side herbage baffled description. From some meadow near came the "crek, crek" of the landrail—less common, alas! than of old—the note of the snipe, the wailing cry of the pewit, the "coo" of the turtle-dove, were punctuated with the querulous gutturals of the moorhen, shyly under cover in the sedges. Presently a small pale olive rose from the surface and came drifting down the wind, then another and another, escaping their water-enemies below only, too often, to be snapped up by the screeching swifts that found them out too soon. Then, in the very neck of the run, a fish put up, and the serious business of the evening began.

The fly on the cast was a Tup's Indispensable, then the latest invention of an ingenious West-Country angler,* and, when the red spinner is up, a very killing fly, but the fish, continuing to feed, would have none of him. Nor was the Red Quill to his liking, but the first cast of a Ginger Quill on No. 00, covering him correctly, brought him up, and he fastened. For a second he hesitated, then ripped the line from the shrieking reel in an upward rush, leapt into the air, and was off.

By this time the sun's lower limb was resting on the opposite hill, and the wind should have dropped dead. But still it came with a certain bite of chill down the valley from the northward. Yet, in spite of cold, the long, fleshy forest fly vied with the mosquito in assaults upon the unprotected portions of the angler, and moths and sedges began to creep out and flit from flower to flower. Two other fish putting up in the next hundred yards were missed, and a small one was landed and returned. Then, as dusk drew on, the fly was changed for a large Orange Quill on a No. 2 hook.

A good fish was rising steadily, though not rapidly, in the next bend, but the Orange Quill, offered from perhaps too short a range, set him down with great suddenness. A shy fish! So was the next found rising, for he did not wait even the preliminary wave of the rod to cease from his impetuous and greedy feeding.

* The late Mr. R. S. Austin of Tiverton.

Perhaps the necessary wading through the boggy margin to get near enough to the water for an effective cast sent over him a wave that put him down.

The next hundred yards provided no opportunity for the angler, but at the end of them the sedgy screen ceased suddenly, and it was possible to approach the shy quarry with a horizontal cast. Over a bank of weed trailing near the surface an underwater movement seemed to indicate a fish of some sort. The fly, an Orange Sedge on a No. 2 hook, dropped lightly on the right spot, with a line behind it slack enough to let it pass well over the fish before the inevitable drag set in. Up came a big black neb. Instinctively the line tightened, but the fish was already hard in the weed, and nothing could coax or force him out. Ten precious minutes wasted, at a time when minutes were priceless, in vain attempts to persuade him, before the inevitable break was effected and a new fly tied on.*

A few yards farther on a snag divided the current, and a foot above it a good fish was taking merrily every fly that covered him. He was not proof against the Orange Sedge, and in a moment he was being led flapping down on the farther side of the snag. Nothing seemed to intervene between him and the landing-net, when suddenly the rod straightened and he was gone. A feel at the hook in the growing dark proved it to have broken at the bend. With difficulty another was mounted, but by this the rise had ceased, and naught was left for the angler but to feel his boggy way back through the eerie meadows to his starting-point, and thence to the village—disappointed to a certain extent, but with the disappointment more than tempered by the amazing charm of this valley of valleys.

* This was before the evolution of the tactics described at p. 230.

CHAPTER XI

ETHICS OF THE WET FLY

In dealing with this subject, I am conscious that I start with a weight of opinion against me among the fishermen of chalk streams. I have known some of them say in a shocked tone, "But that is wet-fly!" as if it were some high crime and misdemeanour to use a wet fly upon a chalk stream. To make my peace with such I want to argue this question out, and test and see what it is about the wet fly which has brought such discredit upon it among the best sportsmen in the world.

It is axiomatic with many that it is unsuccessful upon chalk streams. That is not my opinion, but in itself it is not an objection. If it were unfairly successful it would be another story. The object of fly-fishing, whether wet or dry, is the catching of trout, not anyhow, but by means refined, clean, delicate, artistic, and sportsmanlike in the sense that they are fair to the quarry and fair to the brother angler. There can be no doubt that the dry fly honestly fulfils all these conditions. Let us see where the wet fly fails.

It is said the wet-fly man's game is a duffer's game, which needs neither knowledge nor any skill beyond enough to cast a long line downstream or across and down; that it leads to a raking of the water, often with two or three flies; that it leads to the pricking and scaring of many fish, to the catching of many undersized trout, and to the undue disturbance of long stretches of water, to the detriment of the nerves of the fish and the sport of other anglers. I am quite willing to accept all this and to eliminate from the legitimate all wet-fly fishing which could come under this description.

What is left to the wet-fly angler? I venture to say a mighty pretty, delicate, and delightful art which resembles dry-fly fishing in that the fly is cast upstream or across, to individual fish, or to places where it is reasonable to expect that a fish of suitable proportions may be found, and differs from dry-fly fishing only in the amount of material used in the dressing of the fly, in the force with which that fly is cast, and in the extreme subtlety of the indications frequently attending the taking of the fly by the fish, compared to which there is a painful obviousness in the taking of the dry fly. Add to this that it provides means for the circumventing of bulgers and feeders on larvæ, that it furnishes sport on those numerous occasions when trout are in position and probably feeding under water without ever breaking the surface, and generally widens the opportunities of sport for the man who cannot be always on the spot to seize the best opportunities afforded by a rise of trout to the floating fly.

Is this method open to any of the objections attending the downstream raking we concur in condemning? Is it a duffer's game? Is it easier than dry-fly fishing? Try and see. Does it lead to the pricking and scaring of many fish which follow a dragging fly? No. Does it unduly disturb long stretches of water to the detriment of the brother angler? Why, it is as easy to spend an afternoon on a hundred yards as it is in the purest cult of the dry fly.

If the trout are feeding, I for one fail to see why they may legitimately be fished for if they are taking a small proportion of their food on the surface, but not if they are taking all, or practically all, of it underneath. There is a sentence from Francis Francis quoted with approval by Mr. F. M. Halford, which runs as follows:

"The judicious and perfect application of dry, wet, and mid-water fly-fishing stamps the finished fly-fisher with the hall-mark of efficiency."*

Nothing could be more just if one reads it with reference to all streams, whether chalk streams or otherwise; but to read it distributively so that only the dry fly may be used on chalk streams, and only the wet fly on other streams, seems an unnecessary renunciation of opportunity; while to read it as meaning that only the dry fly may be used on chalk streams, while wet or dry fly may be legitimately used on others, carries its own condemnation in logic.

Mr. F. M. Halford, with every desire to be absolutely fair, has, I think, in Chapter II. of "Dry-Fly Fishing in Theory and Practice," done more than any other man to discredit the wet fly on chalk streams, by the implications, first, that the principle of the dry-fly method—viz., the casting of the fly to a feeding fish in position—is not applicable to the wet-fly method, and, secondly, that on the stillest days, with the hottest sun and the clearest water, the wet fly is utterly hopeless. On both these points I respectfully join issue with him.

On all that his book contains on the positive side about the dry fly I am in practical agreement. But if the reader considers the rods, the lines, and the flies, that Mr. Halford recommends, he will see that they are utterly unsuited to wet-fly fishing, and it would not be surprising that no success attends them when used for wet-fly work. But if I am right—and I am—in asserting that, given reasonably suitable gear, the wet fly *may* be cast upstream in chalk streams to a feeding fish in position (whether surface feeding or not is, I submit, irrelevant), and that on its day—and there are many such in the season—it will kill fish alike in the hottest, brightest, and stillest weather, and on days and in places and conditions where the dry fly is hopeless, and also in the roughest of weather, then I may claim that it is an art worthy to stand beside the art of the dry fly as a supplementary resource

* "Dry-Fly Fishing in Theory and Practice," p. 38 (1889).

of the angler that is at once fair, sportsmanlike, and capable of adding immensely to his enjoyment, his sport, and his opportunities for using the highest skill, not inferior in any sense (except in the matter of the avoidance of drag) to that exercised by the dry-fly expert.

CHAPTER XII

APOLOGIA

HAVING read through the foregoing pages, I am (indeed, I could hardly fail to be) conscious that I have written dogmatically, that I have used the first person singular with some freedom—more freedom than I had supposed. But I am not going to change it. What I had to say, stretched over a period of years, has been too strong for me. I wanted to elaborate a system, and all I have done is to tell my personal experiences in search of a system. If I have written positively, I would not have it supposed that I claim to be a master of angling, or that I do not incur by the water-side my full share—perhaps more than my full share—of mistakes, tangles, bungles, disasters. But, for all that, I claim to be entitled to speak positively of the things which I have tried and tested for myself and know of my own knowledge. No man can really know either these same things or any other things by reading them in a book or by accepting them upon any authority, whether it be that of Mr. F. M. Halford or another.

Nothing presents itself to any two minds in an identical light. Each sees the multicoloured facets of truth from a different angle. No experience is the same to two diverse idiosyncrasies, and the only help which the writing of a book of this kind can be to others is, not in the laying down of rules, not in the preaching or advocating of systems, not in teaching that which the writer has beaten out by his own experience, but in hints which start or help trains of observation or inquiry in the reader's mind, so as to stimulate him to work out, and prove, by personal thought and experiment, to make his own, the conclusions which his own personality is capable of drawing from the test.

In this way only is progress possible. In this, and in doing something to assure that, in the new learning and in the new systems which come along, that which is of value in the systems of the past shall not be forgotten, but shall be transmuted to the uses of the present and the future, is all the justification I can plead for the foregoing pages.

In giving records of my own experience by the water-side rather than in laying down a system, I am not asking others to do as I do because I say it, or to accept anything from me. I would have no weight allowed by any man to tradition or authority until it is proved by himself; no man's words accepted as final because they are his; everything questioned, tested, and brought to the dock of practical experience. If I have ventured, indirectly, to preach at all, the sum of my preaching is not a system, a method, but an attitude of mind—the importance of being earnest, the power of faith, the observant eye, the unfettered judgment, independence of tradition, and, above all, the inquiring mind.

With these words I commit my pages to the judgment or kindness of my brother anglers with a cordial

"TIGHT LINES."

EXPLICIT.